THE ULTIMATE EUROMILLIONS PLAYBOOK

Course for understanding lottery and improving playing odds

COPYRIGHT © 2024 KRIKOS TERRA. ALL RIGHTS RESERVED

Legal Disclaimer

1. **No Guarantee of Winnings**: This course's content is intended solely for educational and recreational purposes. There is no assurance that applying the methods and strategies provided will lead to a lottery prize win.
2. **Risk of Loss**: Participating in lottery games involves inherent risks. You acknowledge that you may lose the money you spend on lottery tickets. We do not assume

any responsibility for any losses incurred while using the information provided in this course.
3. **Responsible Play**: We encourage responsible play and advise participants to set a budget and stick to it. Do not spend more on lottery tickets than you can afford to lose.
4. **Age and Legal Restrictions**: You must be of legal age to participate in lottery games as per your local laws. Ensure that playing the lottery is legal in your jurisdiction before using any of the strategies discussed in this course.
5. **No Financial Advice**: The content of this course does not constitute financial advice. For any financial decisions, consult with a professional advisor.
6. **Accuracy of Information**: While we strive to provide accurate and up-to-date information, we do not warrant or make any representations regarding the accuracy or completeness of any information provided. Lottery rules and regulations may change, and it is your responsibility to stay informed about the rules governing the lotteries you play.
7. **Third-Party Links and Content**: This course may contain links to third-party websites or resources. We are not responsible for the content or accuracy of these external sites and do not endorse any products or services offered by third parties.
8. **No Endorsement**: This course is not affiliated with, endorsed by, or associated with any lottery organization. The strategies and techniques discussed are independent of any lottery operator.
9. **Use at Your Own Risk**: By enrolling in this course, you agree to use the information provided at your own risk. We will not be held liable for any damages or losses resulting from the use of the information contained in this course.
10. **Modification of Terms**: We reserve the right to modify these terms and conditions at any time. Any changes

will be posted on our website, and your continued use of the course after such modifications will constitute your acknowledgment and acceptance of the modified terms.

MAXIMILIAN MATHIS

CHAPTER 1: INTRODUCTION TO LOTTERIES & EUROMILLIONS

The Euromillions lottery is one of the most popular and widely recognized lotteries in Europe, offering players from multiple European countries the chance to win life-changing sums of money. With its massive jackpots and international appeal, Euromillions has captured the imagination of millions of players since its inception.

Before starting, the reader must be aware that there are some subchapter areas with mathematical formulas and explanations. Some are explained in more detail than others. The chapters with formulas are added for the readers interested in the basic mathematical concepts and can be ignored by the readers that dislike math.

1.1 Overview of Lotteries

Lotteries are games of chance that have been played for centuries, offering participants the possibility of winning substantial prizes based on the random selection of numbers. The basic concept involves players purchasing tickets and selecting a set of numbers in the hope that these numbers will match those drawn in a subsequent lottery draw. The appeal of lotteries lies in their simplicity, the potential for life-changing winnings, and the excitement of participating in a widely recognized and time-honored tradition.

Lotteries are usually state owned and managed, and serve various purposes, from funding public projects and educational programs to providing entertainment and generating revenue for state and national governments. Different types of lotteries exist, including state-run lotteries, national lotteries, and international lotteries, each with its own set of rules and prize structures.

Euromillions is a transnational lottery that spans several European countries, including the UK, France, Spain, and others. Players select five main numbers between 1 and 50 and two "Lucky Stars" between 1 and 12 with hopes of matching the draw and winning the grand prize. The lottery is known for its huge jackpots, often reaching hundreds of millions of euros, which are drawn every Tuesday and Friday evening West European time.

1.2 History of Lotteries

The history of lotteries dates back to ancient civilizations. The earliest recorded lotteries can be traced to China during the Han Dynasty (205–187 BC), where they were used to fund large government projects, including the construction of the Great Wall. In ancient Rome, lotteries were held during feasts and banquets, where guests received tickets and prizes ranged from goods to money.

Lotteries gained prominence in Europe during the Renaissance. The first recorded European lottery was held in 1446 in Milan to finance a war against Venice. By the 16th century, lotteries had spread across Europe, becoming particularly popular in the Netherlands and England. In 1569, Queen Elizabeth I chartered the first English state lottery to raise funds for public works, including the repair of harbors and fortifications.

The modern lottery system began to take shape in the 19th and 20th centuries, with the establishment of state and national lotteries aimed at generating revenue for public purposes. Today, lotteries are a global phenomenon, with millions of people participating in various lottery games, including the well-known 6/49 and EuroMillions formats.

Launched on February 7, 2004, the Euromillions lottery was initially introduced by three founding countries: France, Spain, and the United Kingdom. Over time, other European nations joined, expanding the reach and popularity of the lottery. Since its launch, Euromillions has produced some of the largest lottery jackpots in history, making it a significant part of the European gambling landscape.

As of now, the participating countries in the Euromillions lottery are:

Austria

Belgium

France

Ireland

Luxembourg

Portugal

Spain

Switzerland

United Kingdom

These countries collectively contribute to the prize pool, making Euromillions one of the largest and most popular lotteries in Europe.

You can cash in a winning Euromillions ticket even if you are not a resident of one of the participating countries. However, there are some important points to consider:

Claiming the Prize: You must <u>claim the prize in the country where you purchased the ticket</u>. For example, if you bought the ticket in France, you would need to claim the prize in France, regardless of your country of residence.

Some countries allow online ticket purchases through authorized lottery websites, and if you win through such a platform, the prize may be transferred to you electronically, depending on the rules of the site.

Tax Implications: Taxes on lottery winnings vary by country. Some Euromillions countries do not tax lottery winnings, while others do. Additionally, if your home country taxes foreign income, you may need to declare your winnings and pay taxes on them.

It's important to check both the country where you purchased the ticket and your home country's tax laws to understand the full tax implications.

Identification Requirements: You will likely need to provide identification to claim your prize, and this will be done in the country where the ticket has been purchased. Depending on the amount won, this could involve visiting in person or submitting documentation.

Time Limits: There are time limits for claiming Euromillions prizes, which are different country by country. If you're not a resident of the country where the ticket has been purchased, it's crucial to be aware of these deadlines.

In summary, non-residents can claim Euromillions winnings, but they must do so in the country where the ticket has been purchased, while also taking into consideration the local tax laws, identification requirements, and time limits for claiming prizes.

1.3 The Global Lottery Landscape

Lotteries operate in different forms around the world, reflecting cultural and regulatory differences. State lotteries are common in the United States, where individual states run their own lotteries to support education, infrastructure, and other public services. Examples include the Powerball and Mega Millions lotteries.

In Europe, national lotteries are prevalent, with countries like the United Kingdom, France, and Spain operating their own national games. EuroMillions is a popular transnational lottery played across multiple European countries, offering substantial jackpots and cross-border participation.

Lotteries are also popular in Asia, Africa, and Latin America, each with unique formats and objectives. Despite regional differences, the fundamental principles of lotteries remain the same: players select numbers, purchase tickets, and hope to match their numbers with those drawn to win prizes.

Here's some comparison of the Euromillions lottery to other major global lotteries based on various factors:

Odds of Winning

Euromillions: The odds of winning the jackpot are 1 in 139,838,160. To win any of the smallest prizes, the odds are 1 in 13.

Powerball (USA): The odds of winning the jackpot are 1 in 292,201,338. Overall odds of winning any prize are approximately 1 in 24.9.

Mega Millions (USA): The odds of winning the jackpot are 1 in 302,575,350. Overall odds of winning any prize are approximately 1 in 24.

Lotto (UK): The odds of winning the jackpot are 1 in

45,057,474. Overall odds of winning any prize are 1 in 9.3.

SuperEnalotto (Italy): The odds of winning the jackpot are 1 in 622,614,630. Overall odds of winning any prize are approximately 1 in 20.

Jackpot Size

Euromillions: The jackpot starts at €17 million and can roll over up to a maximum of €240 million (sometimes, for big jackpots not won for multiple draws in a row, the sum is distributed to lower categories and these games are very interesting to players, from winnings perspective).

Powerball (USA): The jackpot starts at $20 million and can grow to over $1 billion. There is no maximum cap.

Mega Millions (USA): The jackpot starts at $20 million and can also grow to over $1 billion. There is no maximum cap.

Lotto (UK): The jackpot starts at £2 million and can grow to a maximum of £22 million.

SuperEnalotto (Italy): The jackpot starts at €1.3 million and can grow to over €200 million. There is no maximum cap.

Prize Structure

Euromillions: There are 13 prize tiers, ranging from the jackpot (matching 5 numbers and 2 Lucky Stars) to smaller prizes for matching 2 numbers.

Powerball (USA): There are 9 prize tiers, ranging from the jackpot (matching 5 numbers and the Powerball) to a prize for matching just the Powerball.

Mega Millions (USA): There are 9 prize tiers, ranging from the jackpot (matching 5 numbers and the Mega Ball) to smaller prizes for matching only the Mega Ball.

Lotto (UK): There are 7 prize tiers, with the jackpot awarded for matching all 6 numbers, and smaller prizes for matching fewer numbers.

SuperEnalotto (Italy): There are 6 prize tiers, with the jackpot awarded for matching all 6 numbers and smaller prizes for matching fewer numbers.

Number of Participating Countries

Euromillions: Participating countries include Austria, Belgium, France, Ireland, Luxembourg, Portugal, Spain, Switzerland, and the UK.

Powerball (USA): Operates within the United States, with some states participating in multi-state draws.

Mega Millions (USA): Operates within the United States, with participation from multiple states.

Lotto (UK): Exclusively available in the United Kingdom.

SuperEnalotto (Italy): Exclusively available in Italy.

Ticket Price

Euromillions: Ticket prices vary by country but generally cost around €2.50 to €3 per line at the time of publishing this analysis.

Powerball (USA): Ticket price is $2 per line, with an additional $1 for the Power Play option.

Mega Millions (USA): Ticket price is $2 per line, with an additional $1 for the Megaplier option.

Lotto (UK): Ticket price is £2.50 per line.

SuperEnalotto (Italy): Ticket price is €1 per line.

Frequency of Draws

Euromillions: Draws are held twice a week, on Tuesday and Friday.

Powerball (USA): Draws are held twice a week, on Wednesday and Saturday.

Mega Millions (USA): Draws are held twice a week, on Tuesday and Friday.

Lotto (UK): Draws are held twice a week, on Wednesday and Saturday.

SuperEnalotto (Italy): Draws are held three times a week, on Tuesday, Thursday, and Saturday.

Taxation on Winnings

Euromillions: Taxation varies by country. Some countries have no tax on lottery winnings, while others may tax them.

Powerball (USA): Winnings are subject to federal income tax and, in some cases, state taxes.

Mega Millions (USA): Winnings are subject to federal income tax and, in some cases, state taxes.

Lotto (UK): Lottery winnings are not taxed in the UK.

SuperEnalotto (Italy): Winnings are subject to a 20% tax.

The taxation on Euromillions lottery winnings varies by country. Here is a list of the tax treatment for Euromillions winnings in each participating country at the time of writing, for exact tax the local legislation should be verified:

1. Austria
Tax on Winnings: 0% (No tax on lottery winnings)

2. Belgium

Tax on Winnings: 0% (No tax on lottery winnings)

3. France

Tax on Winnings: 12% withholding tax on lottery winnings.

4. Ireland

Tax on Winnings: 0% (No tax on lottery winnings)

5. Luxembourg

Tax on Winnings: 0% (No tax on lottery winnings)

6. Portugal

Tax on Winnings: 20% tax on lottery winnings over €5,000.

7. Spain

Tax on Winnings: 20% tax on winnings over €40,000.

8. Switzerland

Tax on Winnings: 35% tax on winnings.

9. United Kingdom

Tax on Winnings: 0% (No tax on lottery winnings)

Important Note: Tax laws can be subject to change, and it's always a good idea to check with local tax authorities or consult a tax professional for the most current information and any specific details related to your situation.

CHAPTER 2: HOW LOTTERIES WORK

2.1 How Lotteries Work

The mechanics of a lottery draw involve a random selection process designed to ensure fairness and transparency. Players choose a set of numbers within a specified range and purchase tickets that correspond to their chosen numbers. In the Euromillions lottery, players select 5 numbers from a pool of 50 and 2 numbers from a pool of 12.

The draw itself is conducted using mechanical or electronic random number generators to ensure unbiased results. Typically, numbered balls are mixed in a machine and drawn one by one, or a computer algorithm randomly selects the winning numbers. The process is often overseen by independent auditors to guarantee the integrity of the draw.

Winners are determined by the number of matching numbers on their ticket. Prizes are awarded based on the number of matches, with larger prizes for more matches. In addition to the main jackpot, many lotteries offer secondary prizes for matching fewer numbers.

2.2 Common Lottery Formats

6/49 Lottery Format

The 6/49 lottery format is one of the most popular and widely recognized lottery systems. Players select six numbers from a pool of 49. To win the jackpot, a player's numbers must match all six numbers drawn in the lottery. Secondary prizes are awarded for matching five, four, or three numbers. The simplicity and familiarity of the 6/49 format make it a favorite among lottery enthusiasts.

EuroMillions Format

In the Euromillions format, players select five numbers from a pool of 50 and two additional "Lucky Star" numbers from a pool of 12. To win the jackpot, a player's numbers must match all seven numbers drawn (five main numbers and two Lucky Stars). EuroMillions offers substantial jackpots and multiple prize tiers, making it a highly attractive lottery option.

This is how an old euroMillions ticket looks like (when Lucky Stars pool was only 1-11).

Winning combinations are as follows, with example winnings (as appearing on the back of the tickers):

Rang de gain	Bons numéros	Bonnes étoiles	Gain moyen
1	5	★★	Jackpot (min. 17 M €)
2	5	★	200.737 €
3	5		20.851 €
4	4	★★	1.298 €
5	4	★	119 €
6	3	★★	57 €
7	4		39 €
8	2	★★	14 €
9	3	★	11 €
10	3		9 €
11	1	★★	6 €
12	2	★	5 €
13	2		4 €

2.3 Odds and Probability and some Mathematics Behind Lottery Games

Understanding the odds and probability in lotteries is essential for anyone looking to enhance their chances of winning. This chapter will delve into the mathematical foundations of lotteries, using detailed examples from EuroMillions.

2.4 Basics of Probability

Probability is the measure of the likelihood that an event will occur. It ranges from 0 (an impossible event) to 1 (a certain event). In the context of lotteries, probability helps us understand how likely we are to draw a particular combination of numbers.

The probability (P) of an event occurring is calculated using the formula:

$$P = \frac{\text{Number of favorable outcomes}}{\text{Total number of possible outcomes}}$$

2.5 Combinatorial Mathematics in Lotteries

Lotteries are based on combinatorial mathematics, which deals with counting, arrangement, and combination of objects. The most relevant concept for lotteries is combinations, which represent the selection of items without regard to order.

The number of combinations (C) of selecting r objects from a set of n objects is given by:

$$C(n,r) = \frac{n!}{r!(n-r)!}$$

Where n! (n factorial) is the product of all positive integers up to n (Example: 5! = 1 * 2 * 3 * 4 * 5).

2.6 Understanding EuroMillions Odds

EuroMillions requires players to select five main numbers from a pool of 50 and two "Lucky Star" numbers from a pool of 12. The odds of winning the jackpot, which involves matching all five main numbers and both Lucky Stars, can be calculated in two steps.

First, calculate the number of combinations for the main numbers:

$$C(50,5) = \frac{50!}{5!(50-5)!} = \frac{50!}{5! \times 45!}$$

$$C(50,5) = \frac{50 \times 49 \times 48 \times 47 \times 46}{5 \times 4 \times 3 \times 2 \times 1} = 2,118,760$$

Next, calculate the combinations for the Lucky Stars:

$$C(12,2) = \frac{12!}{2!(12-2)!} = \frac{12 \times 11}{2 \times 1} = 66$$

The total number of combinations for EuroMillions is the product of these two results:

$$\text{Total combinations} = C(50,5) \times C(12,2) = 2,118,760 \times 66 = 139,838,160$$

Thus, the probability of winning the EuroMillions jackpot is:

$$P(\text{winning}) = \frac{1}{139{,}838{,}160}$$

This translates to approximately 1 in 140 million.

2.7 Example: Calculating Smaller Prizes

Lotteries often offer secondary prizes for matching fewer numbers. Let's examine the odds of winning smaller prizes in EuroMillions.

- **Matching 5 main numbers:** We calculate the combinations for the main numbers only:

$$P(\text{matching } 5) = \frac{1}{2{,}118{,}760}$$

This translates to approximately 1 in 2.1 million.

- **Matching 4 main numbers and 2 Lucky Stars:** We select 4 correct main numbers from 5 and 1 incorrect number from the remaining 45, along with both Lucky Stars:

$C(5,4) \times C(45,1) \times C(12,2) = 5 \times 45 \times 66 = 14{,}850$

The total combinations are the same (139,838,160), so the probability is:

$P(\text{matching } 4 + 2) = \frac{14{,}850}{139{,}838{,}160} \approx 1 \text{ in } 9{,}407$

Interesting note:

If all combinations have the same probability, why do we say that *"Sequential numbers (e.g. 1, 2, 3) are less likely to be drawn"*?

The mathematics behind the statement "*Sequential numbers (e.g., 1, 2, 3) are less likely to be drawn*" involves probability theory and combinatorial mathematics. Let's try to describe it as simply as possible.

In a lottery game where players choose numbers from a predetermined range, such as selecting six numbers from 1 to 50 in Euromillions lottery, each number has an equal chance of being drawn in any given draw. Therefore, the probability of any specific number being drawn is 1/50 in this example.

When we talk about sequential numbers like 1, 2, 3, the probability of this specific sequence being drawn is much lower than the probability of any sequence of 3 individual numbers being drawn. This is because the combination of specific sequential numbers represents only one out of many possible combinations of numbers.

To calculate the probability of drawing a specific sequential sequence (e.g., 1, 2, 3), we need to consider the total number of possible combinations and the number of combinations that include the sequential sequence.

To calculate the number of combinations that include the sequential sequence 1, 2, 3, we need to consider that the sequence can start from any of the first four numbers (1, 2, 3, 4) and then be followed by three other numbers from the remaining 46 numbers (since we've already used three numbers in the sequence). Therefore, the number of combinations with the sequential sequence 1, 2, 3 is 4×C(46,3).

The probability of drawing the sequential sequence 1, 2, 3 is then calculated as the ratio of the number of combinations with the sequence to the total number of possible combinations. Given 5 numbers drawn, the number of ways to select 3 numbers out of 5 is:

$$\binom{5}{3} = \frac{5!}{3!(5-3)!} = \frac{5 \times 4 \times 3}{3 \times 2 \times 1} = 10$$

Let's analyze the number of possible sequences of 3 consecutive numbers from the 5 numbers drawn.

If you have 5 numbers, the possible sequential 3-number combinations are:

1, 2, 3

2, 3, 4

3, 4, 5

So, there are 3 sequential 3-number combinations possible. The probability of getting any one specific sequential combination of 3 numbers out of the 5 drawn is:

$$\text{Probability of sequential combination} = \frac{\text{Number of sequential combinations}}{\text{Total number of 3-number combinations}}$$

The remaining combinations (those that are not sequential) are:

$$\text{Number of non-sequential combinations} = 10 - 3 = 7$$

- The probability of drawing a sequential 3-number combination out of the 5 drawn numbers is **30%**.
- The probability of drawing a non-sequential 3-number combination out of the 5 drawn numbers is **70%**.

For the Lucky Stars, the situation is similar from the sequential 7 non sequential perspective:

- The probability of drawing a sequential pair of Lucky Stars is **16.7% (11 out of 66)**.
- The probability of drawing a non-sequential pair of Lucky Stars is **83.3%**.

We can keep in mind that it's more likely to draw a non-sequential combination of 3 numbers than a sequential one, making sequential numbers less likely to be drawn in a single lottery draw. However, it's important to note that over many draws, all possible combinations have an equal chance of being drawn due to the random nature of lottery games (some detailed examples in #2.6).

2.8 Strategies to Improve Odds - in very short description

While the odds of winning the lottery are inherently low,

players can adopt strategies to improve their chances:

1. Syndicates: Joining a lottery syndicate, where a group of players pool their money to buy multiple tickets, can increase the collective odds of winning. While the prize is shared among members, the overall chances of winning improve.

2. Wheeling Systems: Wheeling systems involve playing multiple combinations of a set of chosen numbers. This strategy can increase the likelihood of winning secondary prizes, although it does not change the odds of winning the jackpot.

3. Avoiding Popular Combinations: Some number combinations, such as consecutive numbers or patterns (e.g., 1, 2, 3, 4, 5, 6), are more popular among players. Winning with these combinations may result in sharing the prize with many others. Choosing less common combinations can help maximize the prize if you win.

2.9 Misconceptions About Lottery Odds

Several misconceptions exist about lottery odds:

1. "Due Numbers": Some players believe that certain numbers are "due" to be drawn because they haven't appeared recently. However, each draw is independent, and <u>the probability of drawing any specific number remains constant</u>.

2. Lucky Numbers: While personal "lucky numbers" may add to the fun of playing, they do not influence the odds of winning. The draw is random, and all combinations have an equal chance of being selected.

3. Changing Numbers: Switching numbers for each draw does not affect the odds. Consistently playing the same numbers or changing them every draw both result in the same probabilities.

2.10 The Reality of Lottery Wins and Statistics

Understanding the actual chances of winning can help set realistic expectations. Lotteries are primarily a form of entertainment, and while the possibility of winning a large prize is exciting, it is important to play responsibly.

Interesting to note: Rollovers

EuroMillions often experiences rollovers, where the jackpot prize increases because there were no winners in previous draws. While the growing jackpot attracts more players, the odds of winning remain the same. In October 2019, the EuroMillions jackpot reached its cap of €190 million, which resulted in increased ticket sales and media attention. Despite the high stakes, the probability of winning the jackpot was still 1 in 139,838,160.

STATISTICS for 5/50 (EuroMillions type)

Example statistics how many ODD/EVEN numbers have been generated randomly draws for a set of 5 numbers between 1-50 (as for EuroMillions). We can see some percentage differences in the small number of drawings and in the bigger number of drawings BUT the view is at the same time very similar.

Draws: 539062,
5 Even + 0 Odd: 13380, (2.4820%)
4 Even + 1 Odd: 80610, (14.95375%)
3 Even + 2 Odd: 175675, (32.589%)
2 Even + 3 Odd: 175159, (32.4932%)
1 Even + 4 Odd: 80908, (15.00903%)
0 Even + 5 Odd: 13330, (2.4728%).

Draws: 2500,
5 Even + 0 Odd: 82, (3.28%)
4 Even + 1 Odd: 427, (17.08%)
3 Even + 2 Odd: 817, (32.68%)
2 Even + 3 Odd: 787, (31.48%)
1 Even + 4 Odd: 328, (13.12%)
0 Even + 5 Odd: 59, (2.36%).

!!! Question: If anyone is claiming it can happen sometimes to flip 7 heads in a row, would you believe it?

Amazing mind bending example to help us understand randomness.

Below we have the beauty of random events statistics in a simple example of flipping a coin, with 1/2 probability. The exercise has few steps, please read carefully to understand each step:

Imagine line up 1000 people, give each a coin and ask them to flip it. About half would be heads, the other half would get tails.
People that had tails are asked to sit down.
Remaining ones (about half - let's say 500) flip again, 2nd time.
About half would be heads, the other half would get tails.
Again, the ones with tails (about half - let's say 250) sit down.
Remaining ones (about half - let's say 250) flip again, 3rd time.
About half would be heads, the other half would get tails.
Again, the ones with tails (about half - let's say 125) sit down.
Remaining ones (about half - let's say 125) flip again, 4th time.
About half would be heads, the other half would get tails.
Again, the ones with tails (about half - let's say 60) sit down.
Remaining ones (about half - let's say 60) flip again, 5th time.
About half would be heads, the other half would get tails.
Again, the ones with tails (about half - let's say 30) sit down.
Remaining ones (about half - let's say 30) flip again, 6th time.
About half would be heads, the other half would get tails.
Again, the ones with tails (about half - let's say 15) sit down.
Remaining ones (about half - let's say 15) flip again, 7th time.
About half would be heads, the other half would get tails.
Again, the ones with tails (about half - let's say 7) sit down.

We must all be aware by this time that about 7-8 people that are still standing (out of 1000, less than 1%) had heads 7 times in a row. If they continue flipping, eventually the tail will come. If we redo the exercise, the same pattern will happen, <u>with</u>

<u>different participants</u>. So we know the pattern at a high level, we do not know the details of who will fall into the pattern in which place.

"Exceptions" like this are happening in all random events. This is to keep in mind when playing any lottery. We know some of the patterns and percentages (High/Low, Even/Odd, Averages), we do not know which numbers will form these patterns.

CHAPTER 3: ANALYZING PAST DRAWS

When it comes to lotteries like EuroMillions, understanding the historical data and identifying patterns and trends can provide insights that may enhance your playing strategy. This chapter will explore methods for analyzing historical lottery data and how to identify patterns and trends that could inform your approach to playing.

3.1 Importance of Historical Data Analysis

Analyzing historical data involves examining past lottery results to uncover any potential trends or patterns. While lotteries are games of chance, where each draw is independent and the outcome is random, historical data analysis can still provide valuable insights. By understanding the frequency of certain numbers, number combinations, and other elements, players can make more informed choices.

3.2 Collecting Historical Data

To begin analyzing historical data, you need to collect data from past lottery draws. This data typically includes the winning numbers for each draw, the dates of the draws, and sometimes additional information like prize distributions. Most lottery websites provide archives of past draws, and there are numerous third-party sites and tools that offer comprehensive datasets.

For example, for EuroMillions, you can download historical draw data from the official EuroMillions websites of different countries.

3.3 Tools for Data Analysis

Several tools can help you analyze lottery data effectively:

1. Spreadsheet Software: Programs like Microsoft Excel or Google Sheets are powerful tools for data analysis. They allow you to sort, filter, and perform various calculations on large datasets.

2. Statistical Software: Advanced statistical software like R or Python's pandas library can handle more complex analyses, including regression models and simulations.

3. Lottery Analysis Software: There are specialized software tools designed for lottery analysis, such as Lotto Pro, Lottery Statistic Analyser, and WinSlips. These tools often come with built-in features to analyze historical data and identify patterns.

3.4 Methods of Analysis

Several methods can be employed to analyze historical lottery data. Here are some of the most common and effective approaches:

Frequency Analysis: Frequency analysis involves counting how often each number has been drawn over a specific period. This can help identify "hot" numbers (those drawn more frequently) and "cold" numbers (those drawn less frequently).

Gap Analysis: Gap analysis looks at the intervals between when a specific number is drawn. This can help identify numbers that might be "due" based on their past behavior.

For example, if the number 10 tends to be drawn every 20 draws on average but hasn't been drawn in the last 40 draws, it might be considered "due."

Number Pair Analysis: This analysis examines the frequency of pairs of numbers being drawn together. Certain pairs may appear together more frequently than others.

For example, in EuroMillions, you might find that the numbers 5 and 7 have appeared together in 30 draws, suggesting a potential pattern.

Positional Analysis: Positional analysis focuses on the positions of numbers in the winning combination. For example, you might analyze which numbers frequently appear as the first number, second number, etc.

Trend Analysis: Trend analysis involves looking at how certain numbers or combinations perform over time. This can help identify if certain numbers are becoming more or less frequent.

Clustering: Clustering involves grouping numbers based on certain criteria, such as their last digit, to see if there are patterns in the groupings. For example, you might analyze if numbers ending in 5 (like 5, 15, 25, 35, 45) tend to appear together.

3.5 Example Analysis: EuroMillions

Let's walk through an example of analyzing historical data for EuroMillions.

Step 1: Collect Data Download the last 1,000 draws from the EuroMillions website.

Step 2: Frequency Analysis Count how many times each number from 1 to 50 has been drawn. Create a frequency table to visualize the "hot" and "cold" numbers.

Step 3: Gap Analysis Calculate the gaps for each number, i.e., the number of draws since each number last appeared. Identify numbers with unusually large gaps.

Step 4: Number Pair Analysis Count the frequency of each possible pair of main numbers (from 1 to 50) appearing together. Identify pairs that appear more frequently than expected.

Step 5: Positional Analysis Analyze which numbers frequently appear in the first, second, third, fourth, and fifth positions in the winning combination.

Step 6: Trend Analysis Plot the frequency of the top 10 most common numbers over time to see if their appearance is increasing, decreasing, or stable.

Step 7: Clustering Group numbers by their last digit and analyze the frequency of these groups appearing in the winning combinations.

By performing these analyses, you can gather insights such as below examples:

- Number 17 is a "hot" number, appearing 200 times in the last 1,000 draws.
- The pair 7 and 21 appear together more frequently than other pairs.
- Numbers ending in 3 (3, 13, 23, 33, 43) have a tendency to appear together.

3.6 Identifying Patterns and Trends

Once you have analyzed the historical data, the next step is to identify patterns and trends that might inform your playing strategy.

1. Hot and Cold Numbers: While hot numbers are those that appear frequently, cold numbers are those that appear less often. Some players prefer to play hot numbers, believing they are more likely to be drawn, while others play cold numbers, expecting them to "catch up."

2. Number Pairs and Groups: Identifying frequently occurring pairs and groups can help in selecting combinations that have historically appeared together.

3. Positional Trends: Understanding which numbers frequently appear in specific positions can help in structuring your number combinations.

4. Sequential Numbers: Sometimes, sequential numbers (like 1, 2, 3) appear in winning combinations. Analyzing the frequency of sequential numbers can provide insights.

5. Spread and Balance: Balanced combinations that include a mix of high and low, odd and even numbers tend to perform better. Analyzing the spread of numbers can help in creating balanced combinations.

While analyzing historical data can provide valuable insights, it's important to remember that lotteries are games of chance. Here are some practical tips:

Use Data to Inform, Not Predict: Historical data should inform your strategy rather than predict future results. No analysis can guarantee a win.

Combine Strategies: Combine insights from different analyses. For example, use frequency

CHAPTER 4: CHOOSING NUMBERS WISELY

Selecting numbers for a lottery, whether it's the EuroMillions or other, can be both an exciting and daunting task. Players often struggle with the decision of which numbers to choose, weighing various strategies in the hopes of increasing their chances of winning. In this discussion, we'll explore three primary methods for picking numbers: random selection, statistical analysis, and personal significance.

Random Selection

One of the most straightforward approaches to choosing lottery numbers is through random selection. This method relies on chance alone, with each number having an equal probability of being drawn. Random number generators, both digital and physical, are commonly used to facilitate this process. These generators produce numbers unpredictably, simulating the randomness of a lottery draw. Sometimes named Quick Pick method, it is many times proposed by the lottery provider or by the machine generating the ticket.

Example 1: Imagine using a digital random number generator to select your numbers for the 6/49 lottery. You input the range of numbers (1 to 49) and the quantity of numbers to choose (6). With each press of the generate button, six unique numbers are produced randomly. This method ensures that your selection is entirely independent of any external factors, maximizing the randomness of your chosen numbers.

Example 2: Similarly, for EuroMillions, a physical random number generator could be employed. This might involve drawing numbered balls from a rotating drum, ensuring that each ball has an equal chance of being selected. The process is repeated until the required number of balls (typically five main numbers and two Lucky Stars) are chosen.

Statistical Analysis

Another approach to selecting lottery numbers involves statistical analysis. This method entails studying past draw results to identify patterns, trends, or statistical anomalies that could inform your number selection. By analyzing historical data, players may attempt to identify numbers or combinations that have appeared more frequently or less frequently than expected.

Example 1: Suppose you're analyzing past draw results for the 6/49 lottery. You compile a database of previous winning numbers and perform statistical analyses to identify any notable trends. Perhaps you discover that certain numbers or number ranges have appeared more frequently over time, leading you to prioritize those numbers in your selection.

Example 2: For EuroMillions, you might examine the frequency of both main numbers and Lucky Stars in previous draws. By identifying numbers that have appeared frequently or infrequently, you can make informed decisions about which numbers to include in your selection. Additionally, you may analyze number pairings or sequences to uncover potential patterns that could influence your choices.

Personal Significance

Many lottery players opt to choose numbers based on personal significance, such as birthdays, anniversaries, or other meaningful dates. While this method may not rely on statistical analysis or randomness, it holds sentimental value for the player, adding an emotional dimension to the selection process. However, it's important to note that birthdays and significant dates typically involve numbers within a limited range—months from 1 to 12 and days from 1 to 31. As a result, players who exclusively select numbers based on birthdays may inadvertently overlook numbers outside of this range, such as those from 30 to 50.

Example 1: Imagine selecting numbers for the Euromillions lottery based solely on birthdays and anniversaries. You choose your birthdate (e.g., 14) as one of the numbers, along with your spouse's birthdate (e.g., 22) and your children's birthdays. While these numbers hold personal significance, they are limited to a narrow range, potentially excluding other numbers that could increase your chances of winning.

Example 2: For EuroMillions, players may be drawn to selecting numbers associated with significant dates, such as the day they got married or the birthdates of their children. However, by focusing solely on these dates, players may unintentionally neglect numbers outside of the birthday range. This narrow selection approach could impact the overall diversity of numbers chosen and may not maximize the player's odds of winning.

Considerations

While choosing numbers based on personal significance can add meaning to the lottery experience, it's essential for players to consider the potential limitations of this approach. By exclusively selecting numbers tied to birthdays or anniversaries, players may inadvertently limit their number pool and overlook opportunities to diversify their selection. To mitigate this, players can supplement their personal numbers with additional selections from a broader range, incorporating a mix of birthdays, ages, lucky numbers, and other meaningful digits. This balanced approach ensures that personal significance remains a key factor in number selection while also optimizing the overall number diversity and maximizing the player's chances of success.

4.1 Understanding Lottery Statistics

Whether you prefer random selection, statistical analysis, or personal significance, the method you choose for picking lottery numbers should reflect your individual preferences and goals. While each approach offers its own advantages and limitations, the thrill of anticipation and the possibility of winning remain constant. Ultimately, the choice of numbers is just one aspect of the lottery experience, with the true excitement lying in the anticipation of the draw and the dream of a life-changing win.

Lotteries like the EuroMillions offer tantalizing opportunities to win life-changing prizes. However, behind the allure of jackpots lies a world of statistics and probabilities. In this guide, we'll delve into the statistical intricacies of lottery numbers, exploring concepts such as hot and cold numbers, overdue numbers, odd/even numbers, high/low numbers, consecutives, sum of numbers in a drawing, averages, and differences between numbers.

Hot and Cold Numbers:

Hot numbers are those that have been drawn frequently in recent draws, while cold numbers are those that have been drawn infrequently. Analyzing hot and cold numbers can help players identify trends and patterns in lottery drawings. For example, if a certain number has been drawn multiple times in the past few draws, it may be considered a hot number and may be more likely to be drawn again in the future. Conversely, cold numbers may be due for a resurgence and could be worth considering for inclusion in future picks.

Overdue Numbers:

Overdue numbers are those that have not been drawn for

a significant number of draws. Some players believe that overdue numbers are more likely to be drawn in the near future, as they are "due" to appear. However, it's essential to remember that each draw is independent, and the probability of a number being drawn is the same each time, regardless of its past appearances.

Odd/Even Numbers:

Analyzing the distribution of odd and even numbers in lottery drawings can provide valuable insights for players. While the ideal distribution would be an equal mix of odd and even numbers, deviations from this balance can occur. Players may choose to adjust their number selections based on the historical distribution of odd and even numbers in past drawings, aiming to create a well-balanced ticket that includes both odd and even numbers.

High/Low Numbers:

Similar to odd/even numbers, high/low numbers refer to the distribution of numbers above and below a certain threshold, such as the median or mean of the number range. Players may analyze past drawings to determine whether there is a bias towards high or low numbers, adjusting their number selections accordingly to create a balanced ticket.

Application in Strategy:

Understanding the distribution of HIGH and LOW numbers can be a useful component in forming lottery strategies. Here are a few strategic takeaways:

1. **Avoid Extremes:** While it's possible for all numbers to be in either the LOW or HIGH category, this is statistically less likely. Therefore, avoiding combinations that are entirely LOW or entirely HIGH might be a prudent strategy.

THE ULTIMATE EUROMILLIONS PLAYBOOK

2. **Balance:** Aim for balanced combinations with a mix of LOW and HIGH numbers. Historically, many winning combinations feature this balance.
3. **Flexibility:** Be flexible and adjust strategies based on observed trends and patterns over multiple draws.

Consecutives:

Consecutive numbers are those that appear in sequential order, such as 1, 2, 3, or 10, 11, 12. While consecutive numbers are statistically just as likely to be drawn as any other combination, some players avoid selecting consecutive numbers, believing that they are less likely to appear. However, it's essential to remember that each draw is independent, and the probability of any specific combination being drawn remains constant.

Sum of Numbers in a Drawing:

Analyzing the sum of numbers drawn in past lottery drawings can provide insights into the overall distribution of numbers. Some players may prefer to select numbers whose sum falls within a certain range, believing that these combinations are more likely to be drawn. However, it's crucial to remember that the sum of numbers in a drawing is influenced by random chance, and there is no guaranteed strategy for predicting future sums.

Averages:

Calculating the average value of numbers drawn in past lottery drawings can help players identify trends and patterns. Players may choose to select numbers that closely align with the average value, believing that these combinations are more likely to be drawn in future drawings. However, it's essential to remember that averages are influenced by random chance and may not accurately predict future outcomes.

Differences Between Numbers:

Analyzing the differences between numbers drawn in past lottery drawings can reveal patterns and trends that players can use to inform their number selections. For example, players may choose to select numbers with a wide range of differences, believing that these combinations are more likely to be drawn. However, it's essential to approach such analysis with caution, as the differences between numbers are influenced by random chance and may not accurately predict future outcomes.

While statistical analysis can provide valuable insights into lottery drawings, it's essential to approach such analysis with caution. Lottery drawings are inherently random, and past outcomes do not guarantee future results. While analyzing hot and cold numbers, overdue numbers, odd/even numbers, high/low numbers, consecutives, sum of numbers in a drawing, averages, and differences between numbers can be informative, players should remember that luck plays a significant role in lottery outcomes. By combining statistical analysis with strategic number selection and responsible play, players can enhance their lottery experience while maximizing their chances of success.

4.2 Common Number-Picking Pitfalls: Avoiding Mistakes in Lottery Number Selection

Lotteries are games of chance that offer the tantalizing prospect of life-changing jackpots. While the allure of winning big can be enticing, many players fall into common traps when selecting their numbers. In this guide, we'll explore some of the most prevalent number-picking pitfalls in lottery play and provide strategies to avoid them.

1. Using Birthdays and Anniversaries:

One of the most common mistakes lottery players make is selecting numbers based on significant dates such as birthdays, anniversaries, or other personal milestones. While these numbers hold sentimental value, they are limited to the range of 1 to 31 for days and 1 to 12 for months. By exclusively relying on these numbers, players miss out on the opportunity to include higher numbers, reducing their overall number pool and potentially limiting their chances of winning.

2. Ignoring Statistical Analysis:

Many players fail to leverage statistical analysis when selecting their numbers, instead relying on intuition or superstition. Statistical analysis can provide valuable insights into number frequency, patterns, and trends in past lottery drawings. By studying historical data and identifying patterns, players can make more informed decisions when choosing their numbers, increasing their chances of success.

3. Falling for Hot and Cold or other Number Fallacies:

The concept of hot and cold numbers is a common misconception among lottery players. Hot numbers are those that have been drawn frequently in recent drawings, while cold numbers are those that have been drawn infrequently. Some players mistakenly believe that hot numbers are more likely to be drawn again in the future, while cold numbers are due for a resurgence. In reality, each lottery draw is independent, and past outcomes do not influence future results. Relying solely on hot or cold numbers can lead to poor number selection and missed opportunities.

In lottery draws (or any random events), each draw is statistically independent. Thus, a ball appearing frequently in the recent past **does not influence** its likelihood of appearing again in the future.

However, there are different ways to approach predicting future outcomes. Let's clarify the distinction between two key approaches:

1. **Pure Random Probability (Independent Events)**: Each ball or star has the same chance of appearing in every draw, regardless of past results. In this case, seeing, for example, the ball with number 8 appear multiple times

in previous draws does **not lower** its chances in the next draw because the events are independent.
2. **Trend-Based Predictions**: Some systems attempt to model the behavior as if there were **cycles or trends** in the data, where frequently appearing numbers are thought to have lower chances in the next draw due to their high recent appearance. This is often used in heuristics or betting strategies, though mathematically, it's not strictly accurate in truly random systems.

4. Neglecting Number Distribution:

Another pitfall is neglecting to consider the distribution of numbers in a chosen set. Ideally, players should aim for a balanced selection of numbers that covers a wide range of values. This includes a mix of odd and even numbers, high and low numbers, and a diverse spread across the entire number range. Neglecting number distribution can result in unbalanced tickets that are less likely to match the winning numbers drawn.

5. Using Quick Picks Without Consideration:

Quick Picks, or randomly generated number combinations, are a convenient option for many lottery players. However, using Quick Picks without any consideration or analysis can be a risky strategy. While Quick Picks may offer a diverse range of numbers, they may also produce unbalanced or illogical combinations. Players should exercise caution when relying solely on Quick Picks and consider supplementing them with their own chosen numbers or additional analysis.

6. Failing to Play Consistently:

Consistency is key in lottery play, yet many players fail to maintain a regular playing schedule. Playing sporadically or only when jackpots reach exceptionally high levels can reduce overall chances of winning. By establishing a consistent playing schedule and sticking to it, players can increase their chances of success over time. Much attention must be paid to play responsibly, knowing that all money spent might be lost.

In the world of lottery play, avoiding common number-picking pitfalls is essential for maximizing your chances of winning. By steering clear of traps such as using birthdays and anniversaries exclusively, ignoring statistical analysis, falling for hot and cold number fallacies, neglecting number distribution, relying solely on Quick Picks, and failing to play consistently, players can make more informed decisions when selecting their numbers. By combining thoughtful number selection with strategic play and responsible gaming practices, players can enhance their lottery experience and increase their chances of hitting the jackpot.

!! Very short overview of Trend-Based Predictions

To estimate the standard deviations for the appearance of EuroMillions numbers, we use the Poisson distribution. This is suitable for modeling random events where we count occurrences in a fixed interval and assume a constant average rate of occurrence.

Poisson Distribution Basics (https://en.wikipedia.org/wiki/Poisson_distribution)

For a Poisson distribution:

- **Mean (λ)**: Represents the average rate of occurrence.
- **Standard Deviation (σ)**: Calculated as $\sqrt{\lambda}$.

In this case:

- **Main Balls**: $\lambda = 1$ (each ball is expected to appear once every

10 draws).
- **Lucky Stars**: λ=1 (each star is expected to appear once every 6 draws).

Calculations for Main Balls

- **Mean (λ)**: 1 (a specific main ball is expected to appear once every 10 draws).
- **Standard Deviation (σ)**: $\sqrt{\lambda} = \sqrt{1} = 1$.

1-Sigma Range:

The 1-sigma range is approximately λ ± σ. Thus, it is 1 ± 1, meaning the ball is expected to appear between 0 and 2 times per 10 draws.

2-Sigma Range:

The 2-sigma range is approximately λ ± 2σ. Thus, it is 1 ± 2, meaning the ball is expected to appear between -1 and 3 times per 10 draws. Since negative occurrences are not practical, the actual range is 0 to 3 times per 10 draws.

Calculations for Lucky Stars

- **Mean (λ)**: 1 (a specific Lucky Star is expected to appear once every 6 draws).
- **Standard Deviation (σ)**: $\sqrt{\lambda} = \sqrt{1} = 1$.

1-Sigma Range:

The 1-sigma range is approximately λ ± σ. Thus, it is 1 ± 1, meaning the star is expected to appear between 0 and 2 times per 6 draws.

2-Sigma Range:

The 2-sigma range is approximately λ ± 2σ. Thus, it is 1 ± 2, meaning the star is expected to appear between -1 and 3 times per 6 draws. Again, since negative occurrences are not possible in lotteries, we are looking at the actual range as 0 to 3 times per 6 draws.

Summary to remember regarding Euromillions and to validate with the history

- **Main Balls (1-50):**
    - Mean Appearance per 10 Draws: 1
    - 1-Sigma Deviation: 0 to 2 times
    - 2-Sigma Deviation: 0 to 3 times
    - More than 3 appearances per 10 draws could be regarded as exception when selecting numbers to play

- **Lucky Stars (1-12):**
    - Mean Appearance per 6 Draws: 1
    - 1-Sigma Deviation: 0 to 2 times
    - 2-Sigma Deviation: 0 to 3 times
    - More than 3 appearances per 6 draws could be regarded as exception when selecting numbers to play

4.3. Some statistics considerations & Research tests for drawings of 5/50.

Below tests might require some focused attention to understand but are designed to help the reader see some distributions while analyzing drawings and selecting the numbers to play.

Number of draws: 572364

How many times appeared numbers in previous drawing (when any drawing is taken we can see that the numbers extracted are following the below pattern):

'nr_extr': 572348,
'exist_prev0': 326477, (57.04% - no numbers in previous drawing)
'exist_prev1': 203291, (35.518% - 1 number in previous drawing)
'exist_prev2': 39699, (6.93% - 2 numbers in previous drawing)

The below part could be considered as the exceptional cases:
'exist_prev3': 2824, (0.049% - 3 numbers in previous drawing)
'exist_prev4': 57, (0.0000995% - 4 numbers in previous drawing, 1 in 10.000)
'exist_prev5': 0. (mathematics is saying that if we continue to generate drawings this scenario will come up also)

How many times the numbers in a draw appeared in previous 3 drawings:
'nr_extr': 572348,
'exist_prev0': 106161, (18.548% - no numbers in prev 3 drawings)
'exist_prev1': 198205, (34.63% - 1 number in previous 3 drawings)
'exist_prev2': 161839, (28.27% - 2 numbers in previous 3 drawings) - in all cases like this, it could be that the same number appeared in 2 drawings and the other 4 numbers in none of the drawings.
'exist_prev3': 77148, (13.48% - 3 numbers in previous 3 drawings) - in cases like this, it could be that the same number appeared in 3 drawings and the other numbers 4 in none of the drawings.
'exist_prev4': 23411, (4.09% - 4 numbers in previous 3 drawings) - in cases like this, it could be that the same number appeared in 3 drawings and 1 other number in one drawing, or 2 different

numbers in 2 different drawings or 4 different numbers.

The below part could be considered as the exceptional cases:
'exist_prev5': 4860, (0.85% - 5 numbers in previous 3 drawings)
'exist_prev6': 646, (0.11% - 6 numbers in previous 3 drawings) - in cases like this, it could be that the same 2 numbers appeared in 3 drawings, or all 5 numbers appeared once and 1 of the 5 numbers appeared twice - and all possibilities in between. The detailed analysis has not been done.
'exist_prev7': 74,
'exist_prev8': 3,
'exist_prev9': 1,

How many times the numbers in a draw appeared in previous 5 drawings:
'nr_extr': 572348,
'exist_prev0': 34632, (6.05% - no numbers in prev 5 drawings)
'exist_prev1': 107082, (18.70% - 1 number in previous 5 drawings)
'exist_prev2': 154472, (26.989% - 2 numbers in previous 5 drawings)
'exist_prev3': 137819, (24.08% - 3 numbers in previous 5 drawings)
'exist_prev4': 83748, (14.63% - 4 numbers in previous 5 drawings)
'exist_prev5': 37489, (6.55% - 5 numbers in previous 5 drawings)
'exist_prev6': 12939, (2.26% - 6 numbers in previous 5 drawings)
'exist_prev7': 3333,
'exist_prev8': 686,
'exist_prev9': 129,
'exist_prev10': 17,
'exist_prev11': 1,
'exist_prev12': 1

How many times the numbers in a draw appeared in previous 7 drawings:

'nr_extr': 572348,
'exist_prev0': 11135, (1.94% - no numbers in prev 7 drawings)
'exist_prev1': 48985, (8.558% - 1 number in previous 7 drawings)
'exist_prev2': 100514, (17.56% - 2 numbers in previous 7 drawings)
'exist_prev3': 131616, (22.99% - 3 numbers in previous 7 drawings)
'exist_prev4': 120686, (21.08% - 4 numbers in previous 7 drawings)
'exist_prev5': 83949, (14.667% - 5 numbers in previous 7 drawings)
'exist_prev6': 45667, (7.97% - 6 numbers in previous 7 drawings)
'exist_prev7': 19813, (3.46% - 7 numbers in previous 7 drawings)
'exist_prev8': 7164, (1.25% - 8 numbers in previous 7 drawings)
'exist_prev9': 2139,
'exist_prev10': 544,
'exist_prev11': 111,
'exist_prev12': 22,
'exist_prev13': 3,

Another way of looking at previous drawings (for generated draws similar to Euro Millions) -> how many of the 5 numbers and 2 stars of the current draw appeared in the previous drawings. This looks similar to previous but the way counting has been done is different.

Example to help understanding the difference: In the previous analysis we do not care if the same number appears multiple times in previous 7 drawings, we count each time. In below analysis if the same number appeared in draw 3 and 5 and 6 we will count as "appeared" in previous 7 draws so it will appear as 1.

Analysis has been done on 191994 randomly generated draws.

Checking previous 1 draw (on 191994 randomly generated

draws):

- 'exist_prev1': 68,608, (1 of the 5 numbers appeared in the previous draw) - **35.73%**
- 'exist_prev2': 13,150 - **6.85%**
- 'exist_prev3': 964 - **0.50%**
- 'exist_prev4': 17 - **0.01%**
- 'exist_prev5': 0 - **0.00%**
- 'exist_prev0': 109,231 - **56.79%**
- 'prevstar0': 125,869, (NO Star from previous draw) - **65.55%**
- 'prevstar1': 62,623 - **32.56%**
- 'prevstar2': 3,478 - **1.81%**

Checking previous 3 draws (on 191994 randomly generated draws):

- 'exist_prev1': 75,040, (1 of the 5 numbers appeared in the previous 3 draws) - **39.03%**
- 'exist_prev2': 58,111, (2 of the 5 numbers appeared in the previous 3 draws) - **30.22%**
- 'exist_prev3': 20,122, (3 of the 5 numbers appeared in the previous 3 draws) - **10.48%**
- 'exist_prev4': 3,164 - **1.64%**
- 'exist_prev5': 184 - **0.10%**
- 'exist_prev0': 35,349, (ZERO of the 5 numbers appeared in the previous 3 draws) - **18.40%**
- 'prevstar0': 53,954 - **28.10%**
- 'prevstar1': 102,536 - **53.32%**
- 'prevstar2': 35,480 - **18.45%**

Checking previous 5 draws (on 191994 randomly generated draws):

- 'exist_prev1': 45,790, (1 of the 5 numbers appeared in the previous 5 draws) - **23.83%**
- 'exist_prev2': 69,140, (2 of the 5 numbers appeared in the previous 5 draws) - **35.97%**
- 'exist_prev3': 48,152, (3 of the 5 numbers appeared in the previous 5 draws) - **25.07%**

- 'exist_prev4': 15,454, (4 of the 5 numbers appeared in the previous 5 draws) - **8.04%**
- 'exist_prev5': 1,882 - **0.98%**
- 'exist_prev0': 11,552 - **6.01%**
- 'prevstar1': 95,007 - **49.42%**
- 'prevstar2': 74,015 - **38.53%**
- 'prevstar0': 22,948 - **11.93%**

Checking previous 7 draws (on 191994 randomly generated draws):

- 'exist_prev1': 23,801, (1 of the 5 numbers appeared in the previous 7 draws) - **12.39%**
- 'exist_prev2': 57,552, (2 of the 5 numbers appeared in the previous 7 draws) - **30.53%**
- 'exist_prev3': 65,380, (3 of the 5 numbers appeared in the previous 7 draws) - **34.03%**
- 'exist_prev4': 34,512, (4 of the 5 numbers appeared in the previous 7 draws) - **17.97%**
- 'exist_prev5': 6,958 - **3.62%**
- 'exist_prev0': 3,767 - **1.96%**
- 'prevstar1': 74,563 - **38.78%**
- 'prevstar2': 107,555 - **55.94%**
- 'prevstar0': 9,852 - **5.12%**

Checking previous 13 draws (on 191994 randomly generated draws):

- 'exist_prev1': 2,292 - **1.19%**
- 'exist_prev2': 15,699 - **8.16%**
- 'exist_prev3': 50,973 - **26.56%**
- 'exist_prev4': 77,847 - **40.55%**
- 'exist_prev5': 45,029 - **23.43%**
- 'exist_prev0': 130 - **0.07%**
- 'prevstar2': 164,631 - **85.75%**
- 'prevstar1': 26,559 - **13.81%**
- 'prevstar0': 780 - **0.41%**

Checking previous 17 draws (on 191994 randomly generated draws):

- 'exist_prev1': 409 - **0.21%**
- 'exist_prev2': 5,078 - **2.64%**
- 'exist_prev3': 29,200 - **15.21%**
- 'exist_prev4': 78,382 - **40.80%**
- 'exist_prev5': 78,882 - **41.02%**
- 'exist_prev0': 19 - **0.01%**
- 'prevstar2': 179,469 - **93.53%**
- 'prevstar1': 12,353 - **6.43%**
- 'prevstar0': 148 - **0.08%**

Checking previous 23 draws (on 191994 randomly generated draws):

- 'exist_prev1': 32 - **0.02%**
- 'exist_prev2': 826 - **0.43%**
- 'exist_prev3': 10,259 - **5.33%**
- 'exist_prev4': 57,519 - **29.92%**
- 'exist_prev5': 123,334 - **64.24%**
- 'exist_prev0': 0 - **0.00%**
- 'prevstar2': 188,210 - **98.01%**
- 'prevstar1': 3,751 - **1.95%**
- 'prevstar0': 9 - **0.00%**

A more delicate view to understand how a simple specific scenario can have so many differences in details. The combined view of **HighLow** and **EvenOdd** grouping for 5/50:

493107 drawings have been generated for this view. Here are the results after analysis, each draw has been analyzed for HighLowEvenOdd and grouped as described below:

'1432' = (1 High 4 Low 3 Even 2 Odd): 24964, (approx 5%)

'4132': 22284,
'3214': 24688,
'3223': 51897, (approx 10%)
'3232': 49801, (approx 10%)
'2323': 54522, (approx 11%)
'2332': 51698, (approx 10%)
'4123': 22756, (approx 5%)
'1423': 26825, (approx 5%)
'2314': 26674, (approx 5%)
'3241': 22415, (approx 5%)
'2341': 22736, (approx 5%)
'1441': 10224,
'4114': 10352,
'1414': 13001,
'4141': 9757,
'3205': 4317,
'2350': 3795,
'0523': 4879,
'5041': 1501,
'3250': 3813,
'5032': 3780,
'0532': 4414,
'2305': 4950,
'5023': 3759,
'1450': 1582,
'4105': 1616,
'4150': 1556,
'0541': 1622,
'5014': 1494,
'0514': 2253,
'1405': 2213,
'0505': 346, (less than 1 in 1000 drawings)
'5005': 229, (less than 1 in 1000 drawings)
'0550': 189, (less than 1 in 1000 drawings)
'5050': 205. (less than 1 in 1000 drawings)

Note: Why do the last four groups appear in such a low number of drawings compared to the others? Each combination has the same probability, but there are far less possible combinations that are qualifying to fall in these groups.

The same exercise has been done for 10 times more drawings (4975824 drawings) and we see same pattern in percentages (we can also see that in 80% of the cases we have 32/23 for HighLow or EvenOdd with combination 32/23/41/14 for the other - first 12 rows from below):

'1432' = (1 High 4 Low 3 Even 2 Odd): 250662, (approx 5%)
'4132': 225645,
'3214': 250411,
'2314': 268450,
'3232': 503757, (approx 10%)
'3223': 522087, (approx 10%)
'2323': 548427, (approx 11%)
'2332': 520888, (approx 10%)
'4123': 231166,
'1423': 268972,
'3241': 226827,
'2341': 230097,
'1441': 104722,
'4114': 105022,
'1414': 129628,
'4141': 99020,
'3205': 44553,
'2350': 37944,
'3250': 38084,
'5032': 38107,
'0532': 44783,
'2305': 48963,
'0523': 49592,
'5023': 38090,
'4105': 16814,

'4150': 15484,
'5014': 15269,
'5041': 15430,
'0541': 16715,
'0514': 22355,
'1450': 15804,
'1405': 22546,
'0505': 3298,
'5005': 2057,
'0550': 2014,
'5050': 2141

Separate analysis has been done for drawing random numbers similar to Lucky Stars in Euromillions (generating 2 numbers between 1-12).

HighLow:

- nr_extr: 745,542
- 2 High & 0 Low: 203,007 (approx 27.22%)
- 1 High & 1 Low: 406,418 (approx 54.49%)
- 0 High & 2 Low: 136,117 (approx 18.29%)

EvenOdd:

- nr_extr: 745,542
- 2 Even & 0 Odd: 135,577 (approx 18.21%)
- 1 Even & 1 Odd: 407,035 (approx 54.49%)
- 0 Even & 2 Odd: 202,930 (approx 27.29%)

Consecutive:

- nr_extr: 745,542
- Stars consecutives: 139,309 (approx 18.69%)

4.4 Standard Deviation Overview for lottery of type 5/50

Similar approach can be taken to analyze the 6/49 lottery

or other types of lotteries.

If we sort the numbers that come out from the lottery and assume a linear distribution, we need to find the expected value for each of the 5 positions in the sorted list. These expected values are derived from the properties of order statistics for a uniform distribution.

For a uniform distribution from 1 to 50, the expected value of the i-th smallest number in a sample of size n can be approximated using the formula:

$$E[X_{(i)}] = \frac{i \cdot (b-a+1)}{n+1}$$

Where:

- $X(i)$ is the i-th order statistic.
- a is the minimum value (1 in this case).
- b is the maximum value (50 in this case).
- n is the total number of numbers part of draws (5 in this case).
- i is the position in the sorted list (1 through 5).

Applying this to our scenario:

1. For $i = 1$:
$$E[X_{(1)}] = \frac{1 \cdot (50-1+1)}{5+1} = \frac{50}{6} \approx 8.33$$

2. For $i = 2$:
$$E[X_{(2)}] = \frac{2 \cdot (50-1+1)}{5+1} = \frac{100}{6} \approx 16.67$$

3. For $i = 3$:
$$E[X_{(3)}] = \frac{3 \cdot (50-1+1)}{5+1} = \frac{150}{6} = 25$$

4. For $i = 4$:
$$E[X_{(4)}] = \frac{4 \cdot (50-1+1)}{5+1} = \frac{200}{6} \approx 33.33$$

5. For $i = 5$:
$$E[X_{(5)}] = \frac{5 \cdot (50-1+1)}{5+1} = \frac{250}{6} \approx 41.67$$

The current understanding is that the means for each position in the sorted list of 5 numbers drawn from a range of 1 to 50 are approximately:

1. First position: 8.33
2. Second position: 16.67
3. Third position: 25.00
4. Fourth position: 33.33
5. Fifth position: 41.67

To determine the range for 1 sigma (standard deviation) and 2 sigma deviations for each number assuming a Gaussian (normal) distribution, we need the standard deviation for each order statistic. The standard deviation of the i-th order statistic from a uniform distribution can be approximated, but for simplicity, we'll assume it's known and focus on interpreting the 1 sigma and 2 sigma ranges.

Let's denote the standard deviation for the i-th order statistic as σi(sigma i). For simplicity, let's assume a standard deviation of σi=5 for each position (this is a rough estimate, as the exact standard deviations for order statistics from a uniform distribution are more complex to calculate).

1 Sigma (68% confidence interval)

For a normal distribution, 1 sigma encompasses approximately 68% of the data. The range for 1 sigma is:

$$\text{Mean} \pm \sigma$$

2 Sigma (95% confidence interval)

For a normal distribution, 2 sigma encompasses approximately 95% of the data. The range for 2 sigma is:

$$\text{Mean} \pm 2\sigma$$

Let's calculate these ranges for each position:

1. **First position: Mean = 8.33, $\sigma \approx 5$**

    - 1 Sigma: $8.33 \pm 5 \to (3.33, 13.33)$
    - 2 Sigma: $8.33 \pm 10 \to (-1.67, 18.33)$

2. **Second position: Mean = 16.67, $\sigma \approx 5$**

    - 1 Sigma: $16.67 \pm 5 \to (11.67, 21.67)$
    - 2 Sigma: $16.67 \pm 10 \to (6.67, 26.67)$

3. **Third position: Mean = 25.00, $\sigma \approx 5$**

    - 1 Sigma: $25.00 \pm 5 \to (20.00, 30.00)$
    - 2 Sigma: $25.00 \pm 10 \to (15.00, 35.00)$

4. **Fourth position: Mean = 33.33, $\sigma \approx 5$**

    - 1 Sigma: $33.33 \pm 5 \to (28.33, 38.33)$
    - 2 Sigma: $33.33 \pm 10 \to (23.33, 43.33)$

5. **Fifth position: Mean = 41.67, $\sigma \approx 5$**

    - 1 Sigma: $41.67 \pm 5 \to (36.67, 46.67)$
    - 2 Sigma: $41.67 \pm 10 \to (31.67, 51.67)$

So, the 1 sigma and 2 sigma ranges for each position are approximately:

1. **First position:**
   - 1 Sigma: (3.33, 13.33)
   - 2 Sigma: (-1.67, 18.33)
2. **Second position:**
   - 1 Sigma: (11.67, 21.67)
   - 2 Sigma: (6.67, 26.67)
3. **Third position:**
   - 1 Sigma: (20.00, 30.00)
   - 2 Sigma: (15.00, 35.00)
4. **Fourth position:**
   - 1 Sigma: (28.33, 38.33)
   - 2 Sigma: (23.33, 43.33)
5. **Fifth position:**
   - 1 Sigma: (36.67, 46.67)
   - 2 Sigma: (31.67, 51.67)

These ranges give an idea of the typical spread of numbers in each position assuming a Gaussian distribution.

How do we read this? Let's see stats for random generated draws for 5/50 + 2/12 (similar to euromillions) to see how close we are to theory.

Generated Draw Statistics Calculations (40.000 draws):
Balls means:
Ball 1: 8.44776,
Ball 2: 16.94944,
Ball 3: 25.51184,
Ball 4: 34.001,
Ball 5: 42.4716.
Standard Deviations (1 sigma):
Ball 1: 6.72707299,
Ball 2: 8.58129848,
Ball 3: 9.07709754,
Ball 4: 8.52918982,

Ball 5: 6.7990318.
Calculated sigma ranges - 1 Sigma:
1.72068701, 8.36814152, 16.43474246, 25.47181018, 35.6725682
15.17483299, 25.53073848, 34.58893754, 42.53018982, 49.2706318
Calculated sigma ranges - 2 Sigma:
-5.00638598, -0.21315697, 7.35764491, 16.94262036, 28.8735364
21.90190598, 34.11203697, 43.66603509, 51.05937964, 56.0696636
Stars means
4.32078, 8.65474
Stars standard deviation (1 sigma):
2.68737794, 2.68749987
Calculated Stars 1 sigma range:
1.63340206, 5.96724013]
7.00815794, 11.34223987
Calculated Stars 2 sigma range:
-1.05397588, 3.27974027
9.69553588, 14.02973973

In simple human lines, we can read that the expectation is that the balls will fall into the range 2 sigma most of the time per each position. This means, from all above analysis we could state the following for 95% of the cases in a sorted draw:

Ball 1 should be between: 1-21
Ball 2 should be between: 2-34
Ball 3 should be between: 7-43
Ball 4 should be between: 16-50
Ball 5 should be between: 28-50

As another form of reading it, for each draw, to have **all numbers above 25 can be seen as an exception, draws with all numbers below 25 can be seen as exceptions, draws with only numbers between 16-34 can be seen as exceptions.**

Avoiding these types of drawings when we play, we exclude approx 7 million combinations.

If we want to go with 1 Sigma, below is the calculation:

Constraints and Ranges

- **Ball 1:** Must be from 1 to 15.
- **Ball 2:** Must be from 8 to 25, but greater than Ball 1.
- **Ball 3:** Must be from 16 to 34, but greater than Ball 2.
- **Ball 4:** Must be from 25 to 42, but greater than Ball 3.
- **Ball 5:** Must be from 35 to 50, but greater than Ball 4.
- **Stars:** 2 out of 12 (no additional constraints).

For each ball we have following thinking model for analysis:

Ball 2 choices: Must be from 8 to 25, and greater than Ball 1.

- Depending on Ball 1, the number of choices for Ball 2 will vary. For example:
  - If Ball 1 is 1, then Ball 2 can be any of the 18 numbers from 8 to 25.
  - If Ball 1 is 2, then Ball 2 can be any of the 17 numbers from 9 to 25.
  - And so on.

On average, Ball 2 will have around:

$$\sum_{i=1}^{15}(26 - 8 - i + 1)/15 \approx \frac{153}{15} = 10.2 \text{ choices}$$

We do similar calculation for balls 3, 4 and 5 and we get:

Probability of Hitting the Correct Combination

The probability of hitting the correct combination given the constraints is:

$$\frac{6488448}{139838160} \approx 0.0464$$

So, going with 1 Sigma ranges the probability of hitting the correct combination with the given constraints is approximately 4.64%.

Depending on what risk we want to take and how many combinations we want to play, ideally we want to play something between 1 Sigma and 2 Sigma.

The visual between 1 Sigma and 2 Sigma for numbers to select:

CHAPTER 5: LOTTERY WHEELS AND SYSTEMS

Lottery wheeling systems are strategies used by players to organize their chosen numbers in such a way as to maximize their chances of winning. These systems are particularly popular in games like 6/49 and EuroMillions. While they don't change the fundamental odds of any single combination winning, they can increase the likelihood of winning smaller prizes and provide a more systematic approach to playing.

What is a Lottery Wheeling System?

A lottery wheeling system involves selecting a larger set of numbers than you would in a typical ticket and arranging these numbers into multiple combinations. The objective is to ensure that if a subset of your chosen numbers is drawn, you will have multiple tickets that capture that subset, thereby increasing your chances of winning.

Types of Wheeling Systems

1. **Full Wheels**: This system includes all possible combinations of the selected numbers. For example, if you choose 10 numbers in a 5/50 lottery, a full wheel would generate every possible combination of 5 numbers out of those 10. This guarantees that if the

winning numbers are among your chosen 10, you will have a winning combination. However, full wheels can become very expensive as the number of combinations increases exponentially with the number of chosen numbers.
2. **Abbreviated Wheels**: These are more cost-effective than full wheels because they include only a subset of the possible combinations. The trade-off is that they don't guarantee a win even if the winning numbers are within your chosen set. However, they still significantly increase the probability of winning smaller prizes. Abbreviated wheels are designed to ensure a certain minimum match if a specific number of chosen numbers are drawn.
3. **Key Number Wheels**: In this system, you choose one or more key numbers that are included in every combination. This is useful if you have strong confidence in a particular number or set of numbers. The rest of the numbers are wheeled around the key numbers to create the combinations.

EuroMillions Wheeling Systems

EuroMillions has a different format, requiring players to choose 5 main numbers from 1 to 50 and 2 Lucky Stars from 1 to 12. Wheeling systems for EuroMillions can be more complex due to the additional Lucky Stars, but the principles remain the same.

1. **Full Wheels**: Include all possible combinations of your chosen main numbers and Lucky Stars. This is rarely practical due to the immense number of combinations.
2. **Abbreviated Wheels**: Focus on covering as many combinations as possible with fewer tickets. For example, choosing 7 main numbers and 4 Lucky Stars and creating combinations that cover a significant portion of potential outcomes.

3. **Key Number Wheels**: Select key numbers for both the main numbers and the Lucky Stars. For example, always including certain main numbers and one or two Lucky Stars in every combination.

Example of an Abbreviated Wheel in EuroMillions

Let's say you choose 7 main numbers: 1, 2, 3, 4, 5, 6, and 7, and 4 Lucky Stars: 1, 2, 3, and 4. An abbreviated wheel might look like this:

1. Main: 1, 2, 3, 4, 5 | Lucky Stars: 1, 2
2. Main: 1, 2, 3, 4, 5 | Lucky Stars: 3, 4
3. Main: 1, 2, 3, 6, 7 | Lucky Stars: 1, 2
4. Main: 1, 2, 4, 5, 6 | Lucky Stars: 3, 4
5. Main: 3, 4, 5, 6, 7 | Lucky Stars: 1, 2

This reduces the number of tickets needed while still covering a broad range of possible outcomes.

Advantages of Wheeling Systems

1. **Increased Chances of Winning**: By covering more combinations, wheeling systems increase the chances of winning smaller prizes and possibly the jackpot.
2. **Systematic Play**: Players can track their numbers and combinations more systematically, reducing the randomness of number selection.
3. **Cost Management**: Abbreviated and key number wheels allow players to manage their budget effectively while still increasing their chances of winning.

Disadvantages of Wheeling Systems

1. **Cost**: Full wheels can be prohibitively expensive due to the large number of combinations.
2. **No Guarantee**: While wheeling systems increase the chances of winning smaller prizes, they do not guarantee a jackpot win.
3. **Complexity**: Creating and managing wheeling systems

can be complex and time-consuming, requiring careful planning and tracking.

Wheeling systems offer a strategic approach to playing lotteries. By organizing chosen numbers into multiple combinations, players can increase their chances of winning smaller prizes and manage their play more systematically. However, it is essential to weigh the costs and complexity against the potential benefits. With careful planning and understanding, wheeling systems can be a valuable tool in a lottery player's strategy

5.1 Overview of 9-Number Wheel

A wheeling system involves organizing a set of chosen numbers into multiple combinations to increase the chances of winning smaller prizes. In this example, we will use a set of 9 selected numbers and create a wheel that covers all possible combinations of 3 numbers if all 5 winning numbers are within our chosen 9.

Understanding the 9-Number Wheel

The goal of this wheeling system is to ensure that if the 5 winning numbers are among the 9 numbers you have selected, you will cover all possible 3-number combinations from those 5 winning numbers. This increases the likelihood of winning smaller prizes and potentially the jackpot.

Let's assume we select the following 9 numbers: 1, 2, 3, 4, 5, 6, 7, 8, and 9.

Full Combination of 3 Numbers

Creating the Combinations

Here are all the 84 possible combinations of 3 numbers from the set {1, 2, 3, 4, 5, 6, 7, 8, 9}, ideally the rest of the numbers added to form a line to play should map the most common patthers (32/23 for 5/50 for HighLow and Even/Odd):

1. 1, 2, 3
2. 1, 2, 4
3. 1, 2, 5
4. 1, 2, 6
5. 1, 2, 7
6. 1, 2, 8
7. 1, 2, 9
8. 1, 3, 4
9. 1, 3, 5
10. 1, 3, 6
11. 1, 3, 7
12. 1, 3, 8
13. 1, 3, 9
14. 1, 4, 5
15. 1, 4, 6
16. 1, 4, 7
17. 1, 4, 8
18. 1, 4, 9
19. 1, 5, 6
20. 1, 5, 7
21. 1, 5, 8
22. 1, 5, 9
23. 1, 6, 7
24. 1, 6, 8
25. 1, 6, 9
26. 1, 7, 8
27. 1, 7, 9
28. 1, 8, 9
29. 2, 3, 4
30. 2, 3, 5
31. 2, 3, 6
32. 2, 3, 7
33. 2, 3, 8
34. 2, 3, 9

35. 2, 4, 5
36. 2, 4, 6
37. 2, 4, 7
38. 2, 4, 8
39. 2, 4, 9
40. 2, 5, 6
41. 2, 5, 7
42. 2, 5, 8
43. 2, 5, 9
44. 2, 6, 7
45. 2, 6, 8
46. 2, 6, 9
47. 2, 7, 8
48. 2, 7, 9
49. 2, 8, 9
50. 3, 4, 5
51. 3, 4, 6
52. 3, 4, 7
53. 3, 4, 8
54. 3, 4, 9
55. 3, 5, 6
56. 3, 5, 7
57. 3, 5, 8
58. 3, 5, 9
59. 3, 6, 7
60. 3, 6, 8
61. 3, 6, 9
62. 3, 7, 8
63. 3, 7, 9
64. 3, 8, 9
65. 4, 5, 6
66. 4, 5, 7
67. 4, 5, 8
68. 4, 5, 9
69. 4, 6, 7
70. 4, 6, 8

71. 4, 6, 9
72. 4, 7, 8
73. 4, 7, 9
74. 4, 8, 9
75. 5, 6, 7
76. 5, 6, 8
77. 5, 6, 9
78. 5, 7, 8
79. 5, 7, 9
80. 5, 8, 9
81. 6, 7, 8
82. 6, 7, 9
83. 6, 8, 9
84. 7, 8, 9

Why Use a 9-Number Wheel?

The 9-number wheel covers every possible combination of 3 numbers, ensuring that you have all bases covered if any 5 out of your 9 selected numbers are drawn. This strategy does not guarantee hitting the jackpot but significantly increases the chances of winning smaller prizes. Moreover, it introduces a systematic approach to playing the lottery, reducing the randomness of your picks.

Advantages and Disadvantages

Advantages

1. **Increased Chances of Winning Smaller Prizes**: By covering more combinations, you increase the likelihood of matching some numbers in the draw.
2. **Systematic Approach**: Using a wheeling system provides a structured way of selecting and organizing your numbers.
3. **Comprehensive Coverage**: If the winning numbers fall within your selected 9 numbers, you have a higher probability of winning.

Disadvantages

1. **Cost**: Covering 84 combinations requires purchasing 84 tickets, which can be expensive.
2. **Complexity**: Managing and tracking a large number of combinations can be complex and time-consuming.
3. **No Jackpot Guarantee**: While the system increases the chances of winning smaller prizes, it doesn't guarantee the jackpot.

A 9-number wheeling system in a 5/50 lottery can be a powerful strategy to increase your chances of winning. By carefully selecting your numbers and creating all possible combinations of 3, you can ensure a broad coverage that maximizes your chances of capturing winning subsets. However, it is essential to balance the potential benefits against the cost and complexity involved.

CHAPTER 6: MANAGING RISK AND EXPECTATIONS

Managing risks and expectations when playing lotteries, such as the 6/49 and EuroMillions, is crucial to ensure a healthy and balanced approach to lottery participation. While these games offer the allure of life-changing jackpots, it's essential to understand the inherent risks involved and set realistic expectations to avoid disappointment and financial strain. Additionally, recommending setting and sticking to a lottery budget is a fundamental aspect of responsible play.

Understanding the Risks:

1. **Odds of Winning:** Lotteries like EuroMillions typically have astronomical odds of winning the jackpot. As calculated before, in a Euromillions lottery, the odds of matching all 5 numbers are approximately 1 in 139 million.
2. **Financial Investment:** Lottery ticket purchases can accumulate, especially if done impulsively or without a budget in mind. It's essential to consider the financial investment and ensure that lottery spending remains within one's means.
3. **Probability vs. Possibility:** While winning the lottery is technically possible, the probability of winning is exceedingly low. It's crucial to differentiate between possibility and probability and understand that winning

is highly unlikely.
4. **Randomness:** Lotteries are based on random number selection, meaning each draw is independent, and past results have no bearing on future outcomes. There's no strategy or skill that can predict or influence lottery results.

Managing Expectations:

1. **Realistic Outlook:** Maintain a realistic perspective on lottery participation. Understand that winning a jackpot is a remote possibility and that the primary purpose of playing should be entertainment rather than financial gain.
2. **Focus on Entertainment:** Approach lottery play as a form of entertainment rather than an investment strategy. Enjoy the anticipation of the draw and the excitement of the possibility of winning, but avoid becoming overly invested in the outcome.
3. **Budgeting:** Establish a dedicated lottery budget that aligns with your overall financial goals and commitments. Set aside a specific amount of money for lottery ticket purchases and adhere to this budget rigorously.
4. **Diversification:** Don't rely solely on lotteries for financial security. Diversify your investment and savings portfolio with more reliable and sustainable strategies to safeguard your financial future.
5. **Accepting Losses:** Recognize that losing is an inherent aspect of playing the lottery. Be prepared to accept losses gracefully and avoid chasing losses by increasing spending or playing more frequently.
6. **Community Support:** Discuss lottery participation with friends or family members to gain perspective and support. Engaging in open conversations about expectations and concerns can provide valuable insight and guidance.

7. **Gratitude:** Practice gratitude for what you have rather than fixating on potential winnings. Appreciate the present moment and the blessings in your life, whether financial or otherwise.

Setting and Sticking to a Lottery Budget:

1. **Establishing a Budget:** Determine an amount of money that you can comfortably allocate to lottery ticket purchases without impacting your essential expenses or savings goals.
2. **Tracking Expenses:** Keep track of your lottery spending to ensure that you stay within your predetermined budget. Consider using budgeting apps or spreadsheets to monitor expenses effectively.
3. **Resisting Temptation:** Avoid the temptation to overspend on lottery tickets, especially during periods of large jackpots or when surrounded by hype and excitement.
4. **Self-Discipline:** Exercise self-discipline by adhering to your budgetary limits, even in moments of temptation or when faced with the desire to chase losses.
5. **Review and Adjust:** Regularly review your lottery budget to assess its effectiveness and make adjustments as needed. If you find yourself consistently exceeding your budget, consider scaling back your lottery play or reallocating funds to other priorities.

By understanding the risks associated with lottery participation, setting realistic expectations, and adhering to a predetermined budget, individuals can enjoy the excitement of playing lotteries responsibly. Remember that while the allure of winning big is enticing, responsible play is essential to maintain financial stability and emotional well-being.

CHAPTER 7: GROUP PLAY AND SYNDICATES

Playing in a syndicate, where a group of individuals pool their resources to purchase lottery tickets collectively, can offer both benefits and drawbacks. Understanding these factors is crucial for individuals considering syndicate participation. Additionally, there are legal considerations that syndicate members should be aware of to ensure a fair and transparent process.

Benefits of Syndicate Play:

1. **Increased Odds of Winning:** By pooling resources, syndicate members can purchase a larger number of tickets, thereby increasing their collective chances of winning. This can be particularly advantageous in lotteries with sizable jackpots and long odds.
2. **Cost Sharing:** Syndicate members can share the cost of purchasing tickets, making lottery play more affordable for individuals who might not otherwise participate or purchase as many tickets independently.
3. **Diversification:** Syndicates often select a variety of numbers, which can diversify their ticket selections and increase the likelihood of matching winning numbers. This approach can potentially enhance overall chances of success.

4. **Social Aspect:** Participating in a syndicate can foster a sense of camaraderie and shared excitement among members. Collaborating with others to pursue a common goal can enhance the overall lottery experience.
5. **Reduced Risk:** Syndicate members can mitigate individual risk by spreading it across multiple participants. Even if one member experiences financial hardship, the impact on the group is less significant due to shared costs and winnings.
6. **Convenience:** Syndicate organizers typically manage ticket purchases, numbers selection, and prize distribution, alleviating administrative burdens for individual members.

Drawbacks of Syndicate Play:

1. **Shared Winnings:** Syndicate members must divide any winnings among all participants, reducing the individual share of the prize. This can lead to smaller payouts compared to winning independently.
2. **Administrative Challenges:** Managing a syndicate requires coordination, communication, and organization. Challenges may arise related to collecting contributions, purchasing tickets, and distributing winnings, particularly in larger groups.
3. **Conflict Resolution:** Disputes may arise within syndicates regarding ticket selections, contributions, and distribution of winnings. Clear rules and procedures should be established in advance to address potential conflicts and ensure fairness.
4. **Dependency on Others:** Syndicate success depends on the reliability and trustworthiness of fellow members. If one member fails to fulfill their obligations, it can impact the entire group's participation and potential winnings.
5. **Legal Complexity:** Syndicates may encounter legal issues related to ownership of tickets, distribution of winnings, and tax implications. It's essential to establish

a formal agreement or contract outlining the syndicate's rules, responsibilities, and procedures.

Legal Considerations:

1. **Syndicate Agreement:** Syndicate members should draft a formal agreement outlining the terms and conditions of participation, including ticket purchasing arrangements, contribution amounts, distribution of winnings, and dispute resolution mechanisms.
2. **Ownership of Tickets:** Clarify ownership rights to lottery tickets in the syndicate agreement. Determine whether tickets are held collectively or by a designated representative, and outline procedures for claiming prizes and distributing winnings.
3. **Tax Implications:** Syndicate members are responsible for reporting lottery winnings to tax authorities in accordance with applicable laws. Consult with a tax professional to understand tax obligations and potential deductions related to lottery winnings.
4. **Legal Entity:** Consider establishing a legal entity, such as a trust or corporation, to manage syndicate operations and protect members' interests. This can provide clarity on ownership, liability, and dispute resolution procedures.
5. **Compliance with Regulations:** Ensure syndicate operations comply with local lottery regulations and gaming laws. Research relevant statutes and regulations governing syndicate play in your jurisdiction to avoid legal issues or penalties.

Participating in a syndicate can offer several benefits, including increased odds of winning, cost sharing, and social camaraderie. However, syndicate members must also navigate potential drawbacks, such as shared winnings, administrative challenges, and legal complexities. By establishing clear rules, communicating effectively, and adhering to legal requirements, syndicate members can enjoy the advantages of collective lottery play while minimizing risks and ensuring a fair and transparent process.

CHAPTER 8: ADVANCED TECHNIQUES AND TOOLS

Existing software and apps for lottery number selection and statistical analysis tools cater to players looking to enhance their odds in various lottery games. Here's an overview of some popular options in both categories:

1. Lottery Number Selection Apps:
    - Quick Pick Generators: Many official lottery websites and mobile apps offer Quick Pick generators that randomly select numbers for players who prefer not to choose their own.
    - Number Analysis Apps: Some apps analyze past winning numbers to identify trends and patterns, helping users make informed number selections based on statistical data.
    - Custom Number Selection Apps: These apps allow users to input their preferred criteria, such as lucky numbers, birthdays, or other personal factors, and generate combinations accordingly.
2. Statistical Analysis Tools:
    - Lottery Analysis Software: Advanced software programs

are designed specifically for analyzing lottery data, offering features such as frequency analysis, hot and cold number identification, and trend prediction.
- o   Online Lottery Tools: Various websites provide statistical analysis tools where users can input past winning numbers to generate reports and insights into number patterns and trends.
- o   Excel Spreadsheets: Some players create their own statistical analysis tools using Excel spreadsheets, utilizing formulas and functions to analyze historical data and generate number predictions.

Benefits of using these tools include:

- Increased efficiency in number selection
- Access to historical data and statistical insights
- Customization options based on personal preferences
- Improved odds of winning through informed decision-making

However, it's essential to recognize the limitations of such tools:

- Past performance does not guarantee future results.
- Random number generators may not consider personal preferences or lucky numbers.
- Over Reliance on statistical analysis may lead to misconceptions about winning probabilities.

Ultimately, while lottery number selection apps and statistical analysis tools can be valuable resources for players, it's crucial to use them in conjunction with sound judgment and realistic expectations. Remember that lotteries are games of chance, and no strategy or tool can guarantee a win.

ARTIFICIAL INTELLIGENCE: NEURAL NETWORK ANALYSIS MODEL FOR EUROMILLIONS

Current trend in technology is the use of artificial intelligence. While general consensus, at this time, is that we cannot successfully use Artificial Intelligence to predict the lottery numbers, it is clear that using computers we can get some insights which are difficult to see or calculate with pen and paper.

We will present as an example the code in python that can be used in Google Colab to do analysis based on AI models. More analysis and hyperparameters tuning is needed to achieve a reasonable set of results but this is a good base to start.

Below is the breakdown of code into a series of steps and corresponding areas. We'll create Python code to handle each of the following tasks:

1. **Simulate Lottery Data**: Generate 1000 draws of lottery data.
2. **Prepare Input and Output Arrays**: Create the input arrays based on the specified sums of previous draws.
3. **Build the Model**: Define the neural network model.
4. **Train the Model**: Train the model using the generated

data.
5. **Predict with the Model**: Use the model to make predictions.

We add some validation also:

1. **Data Simulation**: We simulate initial lottery data with a specific seed for training and another seed for validation.
2. **Input and Output Arrays**: We prepare the input and output arrays based on the specified intervals.
3. **Model Building**: We define and compile a neural network model.
4. **Model Training**: We train the model on the training data and add a custom callback for logging.
5. **Prediction Function**: We create a function to predict the balls and stars.
6. **Validation**: We validate the model against new simulated data, calculating the total gains and costs, and keeping statistics on prize counts based on the prize table.

The validation part includes calculating how many times each prize tier was won and the total gain versus the total cost.

Below code could be put in Google Colab and used as base to play with it to advance with the tuning process. The results of the current model on random generated numbers are to be improved.

```
import numpy as np
from keras.models import Sequential
from keras.layers import Dense, Flatten
from keras.callbacks import Callback
# Step 1: Simulate Lottery Data
def simulate_lottery_data(num_draws=5000, num_balls=5, num_stars=2, max_ball=50, max_star=12, seed=None):
```

```python
    if seed is not None:
        np.random.seed(seed)
    draws = []
    for _ in range(num_draws):
            balls = np.random.choice(range(1, max_ball+1), num_balls, replace=False)
            stars = np.random.choice(range(1, max_star+1), num_stars, replace=False)
        draws.append((balls, stars))
    return draws
# Initial lottery data for training
lottery_draws = simulate_lottery_data(seed=42)
# Step 2: Prepare Input and Output Arrays
def create_input_output_arrays(draws, intervals):
    num_draws = len(draws)
    num_features = 50 + 12  # Balls + Stars
    X = []
    y = []
    for i in range(max(intervals), num_draws):
        input_arrays = []
        for interval in intervals:
            start = i - interval
            end = i
            ball_counts = np.zeros(50)
            star_counts = np.zeros(12)
            for j in range(start, end):
```

```python
        balls, stars = draws[j]
        for ball in balls:
            ball_counts[ball - 1] += 1
        for star in stars:
            star_counts[star - 1] += 1
        input_array = np.concatenate([ball_counts, star_counts])
        input_arrays.append(input_array)
    output_array = np.zeros(50 + 12)
    next_draw_balls, next_draw_stars = draws[i]
    for ball in next_draw_balls:
        output_array[ball - 1] = 1
    for star in next_draw_stars:
        output_array[50 + star - 1] = 1
    X.append(input_arrays)
    y.append(output_array)
  return np.array(X), np.array(y)
intervals = [3, 5, 7, 9, 11, 13, 15, 17, 19, 23, 29, 31, 37, 39, 41, 43, 47]
X, y = create_input_output_arrays(lottery_draws, intervals)
# Step 3: Build the Model
def build_model(input_shape):
  model = Sequential()
  model.add(Flatten(input_shape=input_shape))
  model.add(Dense(256, activation='relu'))
  model.add(Dense(128, activation='relu'))
  model.add(Dense(50 + 12, activation='sigmoid')) # Output layer for 50 balls and 12 stars
```

```python
    model.compile(optimizer='adam', loss='binary_crossentropy', metrics=['accuracy'])
    return model
input_shape = (len(intervals), 62)
model = build_model(input_shape)
# Step 4: Train the Model
class CustomCallback(Callback):
    def on_epoch_end(self, epoch, logs=None):
        print(f"Epoch {epoch+1}: accuracy = {logs['accuracy']}, val_accuracy = {logs['val_accuracy']}")
model.fit(X, y, epochs=50, batch_size=47, validation_split=0.25, callbacks=[CustomCallback()])
# Step 5: Predict with the Model
def predict_draw(model, X):
    prediction = model.predict(X)
    ball_probs = prediction[:, :50]
    star_probs = prediction[:, 50:]
    ball_predictions = np.argsort(ball_probs, axis=1)[:, -5:] + 1
    star_predictions = np.argsort(star_probs, axis=1)[:, -2:] + 1
    return ball_predictions, star_predictions
# Simulate new lottery data for validation
new_lottery_draws = simulate_lottery_data(num_draws=750, seed=24)
# Prize table -> Integers = balls, decimals = stars
prize_table = {
    5.2: 15000000.0,
    5.1: 54013.3,
```

5: 5410.2,

   4.2: 309.8,

   4.1: 53.4,

   3.2: 18.9,

   4: 12.7,

   2.2: 5.7,

   3.1: 6.8,

   3: 5.3,

   1.2: 3.6,

   2.1: 4.0,

   2: 2.8,

   1.1: 0,

   1: 0,

   0.1: 0,

   0: 0
}

# Step 6: Validate the Model
def validate_model(model, draws, intervals, prize_table):
    total_gains = 0
    total_costs = 0
    prize_counts = {key: 0 for key in prize_table.keys()}
    for i in range(50, len(draws)):
        input_arrays = []
        for interval in intervals:
            start = i - interval

```python
        end = i
        ball_counts = np.zeros(50)
        star_counts = np.zeros(12)
        for j in range(start, end):
            balls, stars = draws[j]
            for ball in balls:
                ball_counts[ball - 1] += 1
            for star in stars:
                star_counts[star - 1] += 1
        input_array = np.concatenate([ball_counts, star_counts])
        input_arrays.append(input_array)
    X_test = np.array(input_arrays).reshape(1, len(intervals), 62)
    ball_predictions, star_predictions = predict_draw(model, X_test)
    # Validate predictions
    predicted_balls = set(ball_predictions[0])
    predicted_stars = set(star_predictions[0])
    actual_balls, actual_stars = draws[i]
    actual_balls = set(actual_balls)
    actual_stars = set(actual_stars)
    num_ball_matches = len(predicted_balls.intersection(actual_balls))
    num_star_matches = len(predicted_stars.intersection(actual_stars))
    # Calculate gains
    for ball_key in range(num_ball_matches + 1):
        for star_key in range(num_star_matches + 1):
```

```
        key = ball_key + star_key / 10.0
        if key in prize_table:
            total_gains += prize_table[key]
            prize_counts[key] += 1
    total_costs += 2.5  # Cost per draw
    return total_gains, total_costs, prize_counts
total_gains, total_costs, prize_counts = validate_model(model, new_lottery_draws, intervals, prize_table)
# Print results
print(f"Total Gains: {total_gains} EUR")
print(f"Total Costs: {total_costs} EUR")
print(f"Net Gain: {total_gains - total_costs} EUR")
print("Prize Counts:")
for key, count in prize_counts.items():
    print(f"{key}: {count}")
```

The results after running the model for 750 random generated draws are disappointing, showing clearly that the complexity of lotteries cannot be tackled with a simple AI model:

Total Gains: 275.90000000000026 EUR
Total Costs: 1750.0 EUR
Net Gain: -1474.0999999999997 EUR
Prize Counts:
5.2: 0
5.1: 0
5: 0
4.2: 0

4.1: 0
3.2: 0
4: 0
2.2: 0
3.1: 1
3: 3
1.2: 9
2.1: 16
2: 56
1.1: 103
1: 321
0.1: 221
0: 700

ANNEX

I. Patterns that could be analyzed

Analyzing patterns in lottery numbers can be an insightful exercise into understanding random numbers, statistics and probabilities, a good learning experience. Below is a list of 50 different patterns that can be analyzed to calculate statistics about their frequency and repetition in lottery draws.

Number Distribution Patterns

1. **High-Low Pattern**: Count of numbers from the lower half vs. the upper half of the possible number range.
2. **Odd-Even Pattern**: Distribution of odd vs. even numbers in a draw.
3. **Consecutive Numbers**: Presence and count of consecutive numbers (e.g., 23 and 24).
4. **Number Groups**: Distribution across specific number ranges (e.g., 1-10, 11-20, etc.).
5. **Last Digit Pattern**: Frequency of the last digits (0-9) in the numbers drawn.
6. **Prime Numbers**: Count of prime numbers in a draw.
7. **Non-Prime Numbers**: Count of non-prime numbers in a draw.
8. **Repeating Numbers**: Numbers that repeat from the previous draw.
9. **First Digit Pattern**: Frequency of the first digits (1-9) in the numbers drawn.
10. **Number Sums**: Sum of the drawn numbers.
11. **Sum Even-Odd**: Whether the sum of the numbers is even or odd.
12. **Spread**: Difference between the highest and lowest number drawn.
13. **Middle Range**: Numbers that fall in the middle range of

the possible numbers.
14. **Corner Numbers**: Numbers that fall in the corner ranges (e.g., 1-10, 41-50 in a 50 number draw).
15. **Adjacent Numbers**: Numbers that are adjacent in the number range (e.g., 15 and 16).
16. **Pattern Repetition**: Repetition of specific patterns from previous draws.
17. **Digit Frequency**: Frequency of each digit (0-9) in the draw.
18. **Cluster Patterns**: Clustering of numbers in specific parts of the range.
19. **Alternate Numbers**: Pattern of alternating high and low numbers.
20. **Sequential Numbers**: Length of sequences of sequential numbers.

Positional Patterns

21. **First Number Position**: Characteristics of the first number drawn (e.g., always low, high).
22. **Last Number Position**: Characteristics of the last number drawn.
23. **Middle Number Position**: Characteristics of the middle number(s) drawn.
24. **Position Parity**: Parity (odd/even) of numbers at specific positions.
25. **Position High-Low**: High/low status of numbers at specific positions.
26. **Positional Sum**: Sum of numbers at specific positions (e.g., first half vs. second half).

Sum and Range Patterns

27. **Sum Range**: Range in which the sum of the numbers falls (e.g., 100-150).
28. **Range Span**: Span of the range (difference between highest and lowest).
29. **Low Number Count**: Count of numbers below a specific threshold (e.g., below 20).
30. **High Number Count**: Count of numbers above a specific threshold (e.g., above 30).

Frequency and Occurrence Patterns

31. **Most Frequent Numbers**: Most frequently drawn numbers.
32. **Least Frequent Numbers**: Least frequently drawn numbers.
33. **Never Drawn Numbers**: Numbers that have never been drawn.
34. **Repeating Sums**: Specific sums that repeat over time.
35. **Pattern Cycles**: Cyclic patterns in draws (e.g., every 5 draws).

Digit and Parity Patterns

36. **Double Digits**: Frequency of double-digit numbers (e.g., 11, 22).
37. **Single Digits**: Frequency of single-digit numbers.
38. **Palindrome Numbers**: Presence of palindromic numbers (e.g., 33).
39. **Mirror Numbers**: Numbers that mirror each other (e.g., 12 and 21).
40. **Digit Sum Parity**: Parity of the sum of the digits of each number.

Advanced Patterns

41. **Arithmetic Sequence**: Presence of numbers forming an arithmetic sequence.
42. **Geometric Sequence**: Presence of numbers forming a geometric sequence.
43. **Fibonacci Numbers**: Presence of Fibonacci sequence numbers.
44. **Multiples of 3**: Count of numbers that are multiples of 3.
45. **Multiples of 5**: Count of numbers that are multiples of 5.
46. **Multiples of 10**: Count of numbers that are multiples of 10.
47. **Mirror Images**: Numbers that are mirror images of each other (e.g., 13 and 31).
48. **Pattern Length**: Length of the repeating pattern cycle.

49. **Symmetrical Numbers**: Symmetry in the drawn numbers (e.g., 21 and 12).
50. **Unique Patterns**: Unique, complex patterns specific to the lottery rules.

Analyzing patterns can provide insights into the behavior of lottery draws and help identify any non-random trends or repetitions. The analysis could provide hints on possible numbers to include/exclude when selecting numbers to play for a specific draw.

III. Calculations - Standard deviation

We are using standard deviation without explaining how to calculate it exactly. Below is an example of how to calculate standard deviation for your preferred lottery. To calculate the standard deviation of each lottery ball for a lottery where you pick 5 numbers out of 50, you can follow these steps:

1. **Collect Data**: Gather a large number of historical lottery draws. Each draw will provide a set of 5 numbers.
2. **Separate the Data**: For each ball position (1st ball, 2nd ball, 3rd ball, 4th ball, 5th ball), create a list of numbers that have appeared in that position across all the draws. The draws should be sorted as in Ball1 the smallest and ball 5 the highest or reversed, doesn't really matter.

3. **Calculate the Mean**:
   - For each ball position, calculate the mean (average) of the numbers.
   - The mean is calculated as:

$$\text{Mean}(\mu) = \frac{\sum_{i=1}^{N} x_i}{N}$$

where xi represents the value of the ball in a particular position in each draw, and N is the total number of draws.

4. **Calculate the Variance**:
   - For each ball position, calculate the variance.
   - The variance is calculated as:

$$\text{Variance}(\sigma^2) = \frac{\sum_{i=1}^{N}(x_i - \mu)^2}{N}$$

5. **Calculate the Standard Deviation**:
   - For each ball position, calculate the standard deviation.
   - The standard deviation is the square root of the variance:

$$\text{Standard Deviation}(\sigma) = \sqrt{\text{Variance}}$$

Example Calculation

Assume you have the following historical draws (each with 5 numbers, one in each position):

- Draw 1: [4, 15, 23, 34, 45]
- Draw 2: [7, 19, 25, 31, 44]
- Draw 3: [5, 16, 27, 33, 48]
- Draw 4: [9, 14, 22, 35, 46]
- Draw 5: [2, 18, 24, 30, 43]

Step-by-Step Calculation:

1. **Extract numbers for each position:**
   - Position 1: [4, 7, 5, 9, 2]
   - Position 2: [15, 19, 16, 14, 18]
   - Position 3: [23, 25, 27, 22, 24]
   - Position 4: [34, 31, 33, 35, 30]
   - Position 5: [45, 44, 48, 46, 43]

2. **Calculate the mean for Position 1:**

$$\text{Mean} = \frac{4+7+5+9+2}{5} = \frac{27}{5} = 5.4$$

3. **Calculate the variance for Position 1:**

$$\text{Variance} = \frac{(4-5.4)^2 + (7-5.4)^2 + (5-5.4)^2 + (9-5.4)^2 + (2-5.4)^2}{5}$$

$$= \frac{1.96 + 2.56 + 0.16 + 12.96 + 11.56}{5} = \frac{29.2}{5} = 5.84$$

4. **Calculate the standard deviation for Position 1:**

$$\text{Standard Deviation} = \sqrt{5.84} \approx 2.42$$

These steps could be repeated for each ball position to get the standard deviation for each and use the interval when selecting numbers.

5.2 Overview For 12-Number Wheel Combinations Calculation

The number of combinations of selecting 3 numbers out of 12 given is by the same formula and we need to create 220 combinations of 3 numbers from our 12 selected numbers.

Creating the Combinations

Here are the possible combinations of 3 numbers from the set {1, 2, 3, 4, 5, 6, 7, 8, 9, 10, 11, 12}:

1. 1, 2, 3
2. 1, 2, 4
3. 1, 2, 5
4. 1, 2, 6
5. 1, 2, 7
6. 1, 2, 8
7. 1, 2, 9
8. 1, 2, 10
9. 1, 2, 11
10. 1, 2, 12
11. 1, 3, 4
12. 1, 3, 5
13. 1, 3, 6
14. 1, 3, 7
15. 1, 3, 8
16. 1, 3, 9
17. 1, 3, 10
18. 1, 3, 11
19. 1, 3, 12
20. 1, 4, 5
21. 1, 4, 6
22. 1, 4, 7
23. 1, 4, 8
24. 1, 4, 9

25. 1, 4, 10
26. 1, 4, 11
27. 1, 4, 12
28. 1, 5, 6
29. 1, 5, 7
30. 1, 5, 8
31. 1, 5, 9
32. 1, 5, 10
33. 1, 5, 11
34. 1, 5, 12
35. 1, 6, 7
36. 1, 6, 8
37. 1, 6, 9
38. 1, 6, 10
39. 1, 6, 11
40. 1, 6, 12
41. 1, 7, 8
42. 1, 7, 9
43. 1, 7, 10
44. 1, 7, 11
45. 1, 7, 12
46. 1, 8, 9
47. 1, 8, 10
48. 1, 8, 11
49. 1, 8, 12
50. 1, 9, 10
51. 1, 9, 11
52. 1, 9, 12
53. 1, 10, 11
54. 1, 10, 12
55. 1, 11, 12
56. 2, 3, 4
57. 2, 3, 5
58. 2, 3, 6
59. 2, 3, 7
60. 2, 3, 8

61. 2, 3, 9
62. 2, 3, 10
63. 2, 3, 11
64. 2, 3, 12
65. 2, 4, 5
66. 2, 4, 6
67. 2, 4, 7
68. 2, 4, 8
69. 2, 4, 9
70. 2, 4, 10
71. 2, 4, 11
72. 2, 4, 12
73. 2, 5, 6
74. 2, 5, 7
75. 2, 5, 8
76. 2, 5, 9
77. 2, 5, 10
78. 2, 5, 11
79. 2, 5, 12
80. 2, 6, 7
81. 2, 6, 8
82. 2, 6, 9
83. 2, 6, 10
84. 2, 6, 11
85. 2, 6, 12
86. 2, 7, 8
87. 2, 7, 9
88. 2, 7, 10
89. 2, 7, 11
90. 2, 7, 12
91. 2, 8, 9
92. 2, 8, 10
93. 2, 8, 11
94. 2, 8, 12
95. 2, 9, 10
96. 2, 9, 11

97. 2, 9, 12
98. 2, 10, 11
99. 2, 10, 12
100. 2, 11, 12
101. 3, 4, 5
102. 3, 4, 6
103. 3, 4, 7
104. 3, 4, 8
105. 3, 4, 9
106. 3, 4, 10
107. 3, 4, 11
108. 3, 4, 12
109. 3, 5, 6
110. 3, 5, 7
111. 3, 5, 8
112. 3, 5, 9
113. 3, 5, 10
114. 3, 5, 11
115. 3, 5, 12
116. 3, 6, 7
117. 3, 6, 8
118. 3, 6, 9
119. 3, 6, 10
120. 3, 6, 11
121. 3, 6, 12
122. 3, 7, 8
123. 3, 7, 9
124. 3, 7, 10
125. 3, 7, 11
126. 3, 7, 12
127. 3, 8, 9
128. 3, 8, 10
129. 3, 8, 11
130. 3, 8, 12
131. 3, 9, 10
132. 3, 9, 11

133.	3, 9, 12
134.	3, 10, 11
135.	3, 10, 12
136.	3, 11, 12
137.	4, 5, 6
138.	4, 5, 7
139.	4, 5, 8
140.	4, 5, 9
141.	4, 5, 10
142.	4, 5, 11
143.	4, 5, 12
144.	4, 6, 7
145.	4, 6, 8
146.	4, 6, 9
147.	4, 6, 10
148.	4, 6, 11
149.	4, 6, 12
150.	4, 7, 8
151.	4, 7, 9
152.	4, 7, 10
153.	4, 7, 11
154.	4, 7, 12
155.	4, 8, 9
156.	4, 8, 10
157.	4, 8, 11
158.	4, 8, 12
159.	4, 9, 10
160.	4, 9, 11
161.	4, 9, 12
162.	4, 10, 11
163.	4, 10, 12
164.	4, 11, 12
165.	5, 6, 7
166.	5, 6, 8
167.	5, 6, 9
168.	5, 6, 10

169.	5, 6, 11
170.	5, 6, 12
171.	5, 7, 8
172.	5, 7, 9
173.	5, 7, 10
174.	5, 7, 11
175.	5, 7, 12
176.	5, 8, 9
177.	5, 8, 10
178.	5, 8, 11
179.	5, 8, 12
180.	5, 9, 10
181.	5, 9, 11
182.	5, 9, 12
183.	5, 10, 11
184.	5, 10, 12
185.	5, 11, 12
186.	6, 7, 8
187.	6, 7, 9
188.	6, 7, 10
189.	6, 7, 11
190.	6, 7, 12
191.	6, 8, 9
192.	6, 8, 10
193.	6, 8, 11
194.	6, 8, 12
195.	6, 9, 10
196.	6, 9, 11
197.	6, 9, 12
198.	6, 10, 11
199.	6, 10, 12
200.	6, 11, 12
201.	7, 8, 9
202.	7, 8, 10
203.	7, 8, 11
204.	7, 8, 12

205.	7, 9, 10
206.	7, 9, 11
207.	7, 9, 12
208.	7, 10, 11
209.	7, 10, 12
210.	7, 11, 12
211.	8, 9, 10
212.	8, 9, 11
213.	8, 9, 12
214.	8, 10, 11
215.	8, 10, 12
216.	8, 11, 12
217.	9, 10, 11
218.	9, 10, 12
219.	9, 11, 12
220.	10, 11, 12

How to Use Wheels to Improve Odds in Lotteries

Lottery wheeling systems are popular among serious lottery players who want to increase their chances of winning. These systems allow players to play multiple combinations of their chosen numbers, providing a strategic way to enhance the probability of hitting the jackpot or winning smaller prizes. In this overview, we'll explore how to use wheeling systems to improve your odds and provide seven ideas on how to select the numbers to include in your wheel.

Seven Ideas for Selecting Numbers to Include in the Wheel

Choosing the right numbers to include in your wheeling system is crucial for maximizing your chances of winning. Here are seven ideas to help you select your numbers strategically:

1. **Hot and Cold Numbers**
2. **Odd and Even Numbers**
3. **High and Low Numbers**

4. **Number Frequency Analysis**
5. **Avoiding Common Combinations**
6. **Using Personal Numbers**
7. **Combining Different Strategies**

1. Hot and Cold Numbers

Strategy: To use this strategy, analyze recent lottery results to identify hot and cold numbers. Include a mix of both in your wheeling system to cover both frequent and overdue numbers. For example, if you notice that the numbers 7, 14, and 23 have appeared frequently, you might include them as hot numbers. On the other hand, if 2, 19, and 34 haven't appeared in a while, they could be your cold numbers.

2. Odd and Even Numbers

Balanced Mix: Research shows that an even mix of odd and even numbers often appears in winning combinations. For example, in a 6-number lottery, having 3 odd and 3 even numbers is statistically more common than having all odd or all even numbers.

Strategy: Ensure your wheel includes a balanced mix of odd and even numbers. For example, from your set of 12 numbers, choose 6 odd and 6 even numbers. This approach increases the likelihood of covering the most common type of winning combinations.

3. High and Low Numbers

Range Splits: Another strategy involves splitting the number range into high and low groups. In a 5/50 lottery, numbers 1-24 can be considered low, and numbers 25-50 can be considered high.

Strategy: Create combinations that include an even distribution of high and low numbers. For instance, a balanced combination might include 3 numbers from 1-24 and 3 numbers from 25-50. This approach aligns with the statistical trend of mixed-range winning combinations.

4. Number Frequency Analysis

Historical Data: Analyze the frequency of each number's appearance in past draws. This can give insights into patterns and trends that might help in selecting numbers.

Strategy: Use historical data to identify numbers that frequently appear together. For example, if numbers 5, 12, and 37 have appeared together multiple times, include them in your wheel. Additionally, consider including numbers that have shown to appear in winning combinations frequently.

5. Avoiding Common Combinations

Avoid Predictable Choices: Many players choose numbers based on patterns, such as all numbers in a single row or column on the ticket, or sequences like 1, 2, 3, 4, 5, 6. These combinations are less likely to win and often lead to shared prizes if they do win.

Strategy: Avoid common combinations that many players might select. Instead, opt for less predictable patterns. For example, instead of choosing consecutive numbers, select numbers that are spread out across the range.

6. Using Personal Numbers

Significant Dates: Many players use significant dates, such as birthdays or anniversaries, to choose their numbers. This can be a fun and meaningful way to select numbers, but it has limitations due to the calendar range (e.g., days 1-31, months 1-12).

Strategy: If you choose to use personal numbers, ensure you also include numbers beyond the typical date range to cover the entire number spectrum. For instance, combine dates with other strategic choices like high and low or odd and even numbers.

7. Combining Different Strategies

Hybrid Approach: One of the most effective ways to select numbers is by combining multiple strategies. This allows you to cover various aspects and increase your overall odds.

Strategy: Create a hybrid selection process that includes hot and cold numbers, a balanced mix of odd and even numbers, and high and low numbers. For example, select 4 hot numbers, 4 cold numbers, 6 odd numbers, and 6 even numbers, ensuring they are spread out across the number range.

Printed in Great Britain
by Amazon

563ef242-9625-467a-85ce-4f18f380b125R01